Irish Fairy Tales

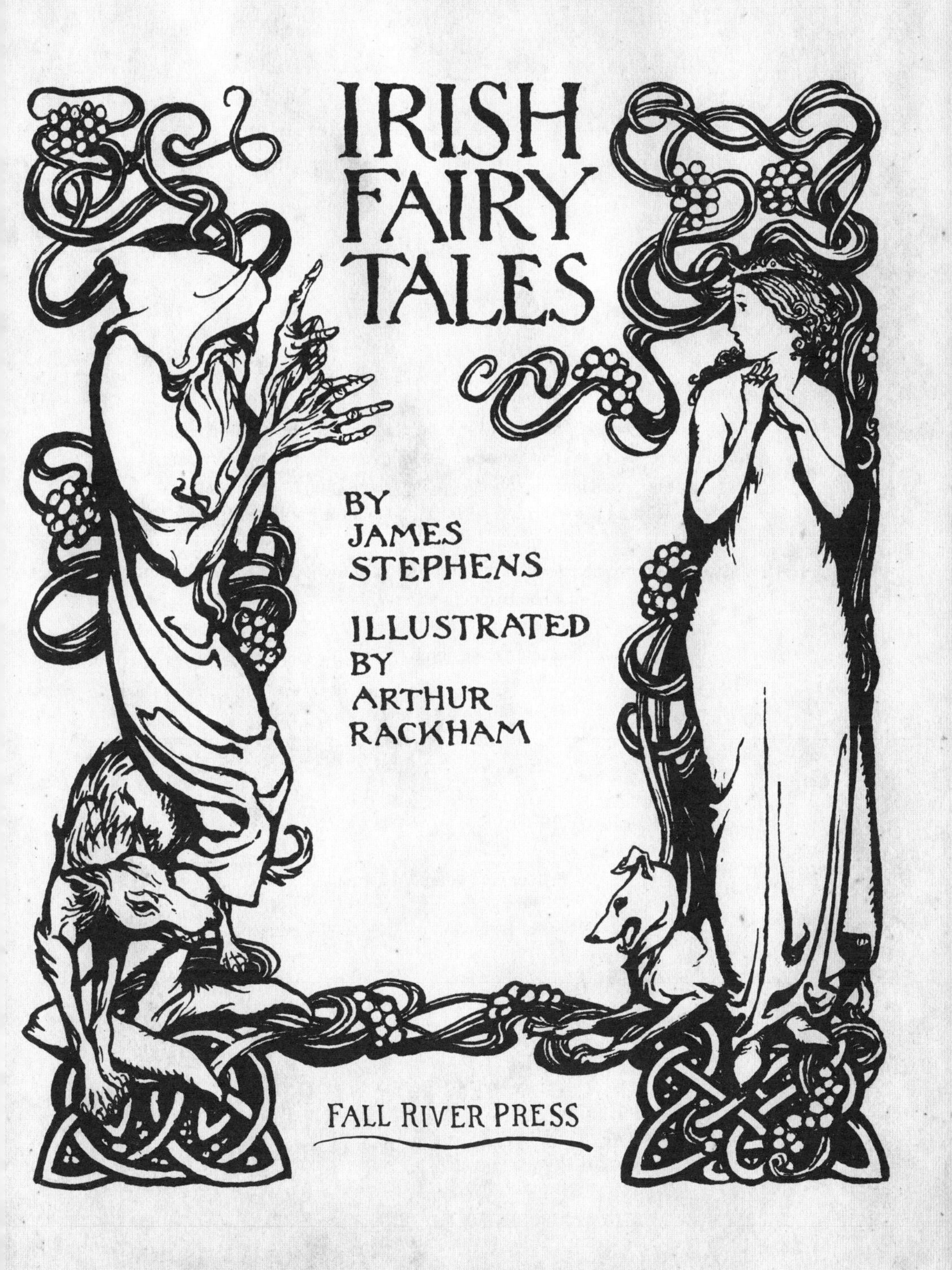

IRISH FAIRY TALES

BY
JAMES
STEPHENS

ILLUSTRATED
BY
ARTHUR
RACKHAM

FALL RIVER PRESS

This 2008 edition published by Fall River Press

Cover and interior design by Christine Heun

Fall River Press
122 Fifth Avenue
New York, NY 10011

ISBN: 978-1-4351-0887-5

Printed and bound in China

3 5 7 9 10 8 6 4 2

To
Seumas and Iris
and to
Helen Fraser

In a forked glen into which he slipped at night-fall
he was surrounded by giant toads

Contents

List of Colour Illustrations

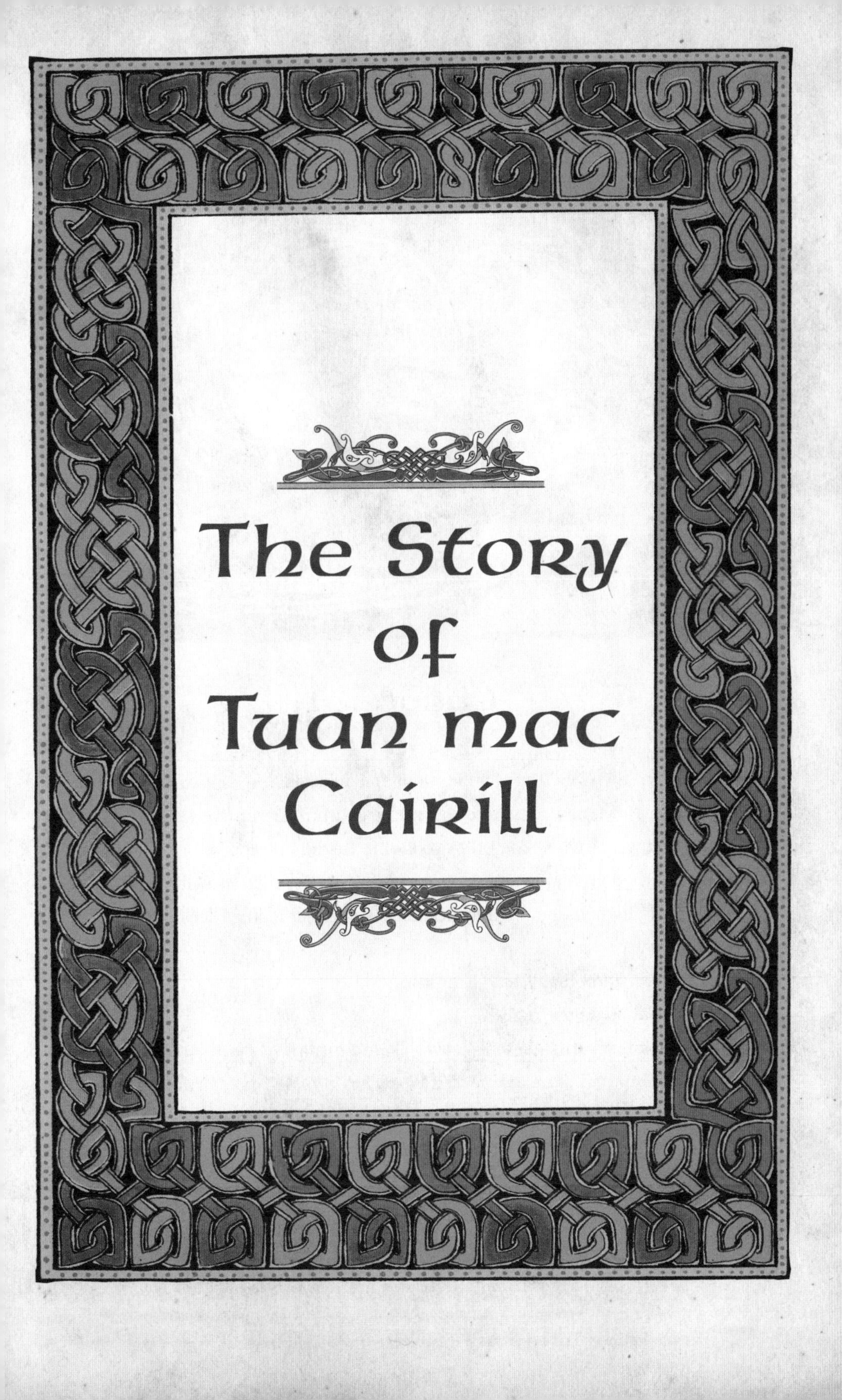
The Story
of
Tuan mac
Cairill

Chapter 1

Finnian, the Abbott of Moville, went southwards and eastwards in great haste. News had come to him in Donegal that there were yet people in his own province who believed in gods that he did not approve of, and the gods that we do not approve of are treated scurvily, even by saintly men.

He was told of a powerful gentleman who observed neither Saint's day nor Sunday.

"A powerful person!" said Finnian.

"All that," was the reply.

"We shall try this person's power," said Finnian.

"He is reputed to be a wise and hardy man," said his informant.

"We shall test his wisdom and his hardihood."

"He is," that gossip whispered—"he is a magician."

"I will magician him," cried Finnian angrily. "Where does that man live?"

He was informed, and he proceeded to that direction without delay.

In no great time he came to the stronghold of the gentleman who followed ancient ways, and he demanded admittance in order that he might preach and prove the new God, and exorcise and terrify and banish even the memory of the old one; for to a god grown old Time is as ruthless as to a beggarman grown old.

But the Ulster gentleman refused Finnian admittance. He barricaded his house, he shuttered his windows, and in a gloom of indignation and protest he continued the practices of ten thousand years, and would not hearken to Finnian calling at the window or to Time knocking at his door.

But of those adversaries it was the first he redoubted.

Finnian loomed on him as a portent and a terror; but he had no fear of Time. Indeed he was the foster-brother of Time, and so disdainful of the bitter god that he did not even disdain him; he leaped over the scythe, he dodged under it, and the sole occasions on which Time laughs is when he chances on Tuan, the son of Cairill, the son of Muredac Red-neck.

Chapter 2

Now Finnian could not abide that any person should resist both the Gospel and himself, and he proceeded to force the stronghold by peaceful but powerful methods. He fasted on the gentleman, and he did so to such purpose that he was admitted to the house; for to an hospitable heart the idea that a stranger may expire on your doorstep from sheer famine cannot be tolerated. The gentleman, however, did not give in without a struggle: he thought that when Finnian had grown sufficiently hungry he would lift the siege and take himself off to some place where he might get food. But he did not know

Finnian. The great abbot sat down on a spot just beyond the door, and composed himself to all that might follow from his action. He bent his gaze on the ground between his feet, and entered into a meditation from which he would only be released by admission or death.

The first day passed quietly.

Often the gentleman would send a servitor to spy if that deserter of the gods was still before his door, and each time the servant replied that he was still there.

"He will be gone in the morning," said the hopeful master.

On the morrow the state of siege continued, and through that day the servants were sent many times to observe through spy-holes.

"Go," he would say, "and find out if the worshipper of new gods has taken himself away."

But the servants returned each time with the same information.

"The new druid is still there," they said.

All through that day no one could leave the stronghold. And the enforced seclusion wrought on the minds of the servants, while the cessation of all work banded them together in small groups that whispered and discussed and disputed. Then these groups would disperse to peep through the spy-hole at the patient, immobile figure seated before the door, wrapped in a meditation that was timeless and unconcerned. They took fright at the spectacle, and once or twice a woman screamed hysterically, and was bundled away with a companion's hand clapped on her mouth, so that the ear of their master should not be affronted.

"He has his own troubles," they said. "It is a combat of the gods that is taking place."

So much for the women; but the men also were uneasy. They prowled up and down, tramping from the spy-hole to the kitchen, and from the kitchen to the turreted roof. And from the roof they would look down on the motionless figure below, and speculate on many things, including the staunchness of man, the qualities of their master, and even the possibility that the new gods might be as powerful as the old. From these peepings and discussions they would return languid and discouraged.

"If," said one irritable guard, "if we buzzed a spear at the persistent stranger, or if one slung at him with a jagged pebble!"

"What!" his master demanded wrathfully, "is a spear to be thrown at an unarmed stranger? And from this house!" And he soundly cuffed that indelicate servant.

"Be at peace all of you," he said, "for hunger has a whip, and he will drive the stranger away in the night."

The household retired to wretched beds; but for the master of the house there was no sleep. He marched his halls all night, going often to the spy-hole to see if that shadow was still sitting in the shade, and pacing thence, tormented, preoccupied, refusing even the nose of his favourite dog as it pressed lovingly into his closed palm.

On the morrow he gave in.

The great door was swung wide, and two of his servants carried Finnian into the house, for the saint could no longer walk or stand upright by reason of the hunger and exposure to which he had submitted. But his frame was tough as the unconquerable spirit that dwelt within it, and in no long time he was ready for whatever might come of dispute or anathema.

Being quite re-established he undertook the conversion of the master of the house, and the siege he laid against that notable intelligence was long spoken of among those who are interested in such things.

He had beaten the disease of Mugain; he had beaten his own pupil the great Colm Cillé; he beat Tuan also, and just as the latter's door had opened to the persistent stranger, so his heart opened, and Finnian marched there to do the will of God, and his own will.

Chapter 3

One day they were talking together about the majesty of God and His love, for although Tuan had now received much instruction on this subject he yet needed more, and he laid as close a siege on Finnian as Finnian had before that laid on him. But man works outwardly and inwardly. After rest he has energy, after energy he needs repose; so, when we have given instruction for a time, we need instruction, and must receive it or the spirit faints and wisdom herself grows bitter.

Therefore Finnian said: "Tell me now about yourself, dear heart."

But Tuan was avid of information about the True God. "No, no," he said, "the past has nothing more of interest for me, and I do not wish anything to come between my soul and its instruction; continue to teach me, dear friend and saintly father."

"I will do that," Finnian replied, "but I must first meditate deeply on you, and must know you well. Tell me your past, my beloved, for a man is his past, and is to be known by it."

But Tuan pleaded: "Let the past be content with itself, for man needs forgetfulness as well as memory."

"My son," said Finnian, "all that has ever been done has been done for the glory of God, and to confess our good and evil deeds is part of instruction; for the soul must recall its acts and abide by them, or renounce them by confession and penitence. Tell me your genealogy first, and by what descent you occupy these lands and stronghold, and then I will examine your acts and your conscience."

Tuan replied obediently: "I am known as Tuan, son of Cairill, son of Muredac Red-neck, and these are the hereditary lands of my father."

The saint nodded.

"I am not as well acquainted with Ulster genealogies as I should be, yet I know something of them. I am by blood a Leinsterman," he continued.

"Mine is a long pedigree," Tuan murmured.

Finnian received that information with respect and interest.

"I also," he said, "have an honourable record."

His host continued: "I am indeed Tuan, the son of Starn, the son of Sera, who was brother to Partholon."

"But," said Finnian in bewilderment, "there is an error here, for you have recited two different genealogies."

"Different genealogies, indeed," replied Tuan thoughtfully, "but they are my genealogies."

"I do not understand this," Finnian declared roundly.

"I am now known as Tuan mac Cairill," the other replied, "but in the days of old I was known as Tuan mac Starn, mac Sera."

"The brother of Partholon," the saint gasped.

"That is my pedigree," Tuan said.

"But," Finnian objected in bewilderment, "Partholon came to Ireland not long after the Flood."

"I came with him," said Tuan mildly.

The saint pushed his chair back hastily, and sat staring at his host, and as he stared the blood grew chill in his veins, and his hair crept along his scalp and stood on end.

Chapter 4

But Finnian was not one who remained long in bewilderment. He thought on the might of God and he became that might, and was tranquil.

He was one who loved God and Ireland, and to the person who could instruct him in these great themes he gave all the interest of his mind and the sympathy of his heart.

"It is a wonder you tell me, my beloved," he said. "And now you must tell me more."

"What must I tell?" asked Tuan resignedly.

"Tell me of the beginning of time in Ireland, and of the bearing of Partholon, the son of Noah's son."

"I have almost forgotten him," said Tuan. "A greatly bearded, greatly shouldered man he was. A man of sweet deeds and sweet ways."

"Continue, my love," said Finnian.

"He came to Ireland in a ship. Twenty-four men and twenty-four women came with him. But before that time no man had come to Ireland, and in the western parts of the world no human being lived or moved. As we drew on Ireland from the sea the country seemed like an unending forest. Far as the eye could reach, and in whatever direction, there were trees; and from these there came the unceasing singing of birds. Over all that land the sun shone warm and beautiful, so that to our sea-weary eyes, our wind-tormented ears, it seemed as if we were driving on Paradise.

"We landed and we heard the rumble of water going gloomily through the darkness of the forest. Following the water we came to a glade where the sun shone and where the earth was warmed, and there Partholon rested with his twenty-four couples, and made a city and a livelihood.

"There were fish in the rivers of Eirè, there were animals in her coverts. Wild and shy and monstrous creatures ranged in her plains and forests. Creatures that one could see through and walk through. Long we lived in ease, and we saw new animals grow—the bear, the wolf, the badger, the deer, and the boar.

"Partholon's people increased until from twenty-four couples there came five thousand people, who lived in amity and contentment although they had no wits."

"They had no wits!" Finnian commented.

"They had no need of wits," Tuan said.

"I have heard that the first-born were mindless," said Finnian. "Continue your story, my beloved."

"Wild and shy and monstrous creatures ranged in her plains and forests"

"Then, sudden as a rising wind, between one night and a morning, there came a sickness that bloated the stomach and purpled the skin, and on the seventh day all of the race of Partholon were dead, save one man only."

"There always escapes one man," said Finnian thoughtfully.

"And I am that man," his companion affirmed.

Tuan shaded his brow with his hand, and he remembered backwards through incredible ages to the beginning of the world and the first days of Eirè. And Finnian, with his blood again running chill and his scalp crawling uneasily, stared backwards with him.

Chapter 5

Tell on, my love," Finnian murmured.

"I was alone," said Tuan. "I was so alone that my own shadow frightened me. I was so alone that the sound of a bird in flight, or the creaking of a dew-drenched bough, whipped me to cover as a rabbit is scared to his burrow.

"The creatures of the forest scented me and knew I was alone. They stole with silken pad behind my back and snarled when I faced them; the long, grey wolves with hanging tongues and staring eyes chased me to my cleft rock; there was no creature so weak but it might hunt me; there was no creature so timid but it might outface me. And so I lived for two tens of years and two years, until I knew all that a beast surmises and had forgotten all that a man had known.

"I could pad as gently as any; I could run as tirelessly. I could be invisible and patient as a wild cat crouching among leaves; I could smell danger in my sleep and leap at it with wakeful claws; I could bark and growl and clash with my teeth and tear with them."

"Tell on, my beloved," said Finnian, "you shall rest in God, dear heart."

"At the end of that time," said Tuan, "Nemed the son of Agnoman came to Ireland with a fleet of thirty-four barques, and in each barque there were thirty couples of people."

"I have heard it," said Finnian.

"My heart leaped for joy when I saw the great fleet rounding the land, and I followed them along scarped cliffs, leaping from rock to rock like a wild goat, while the ships tacked and swung seeking a harbour. There I stooped to drink at a pool, and I saw myself in the chill water.

"I saw that I was hairy and tufty and bristled as a savage boar; that I was lean as a stripped bush; that I was greyer than a badger; withered and wrinkled like an empty sack; naked as a fish; wretched as a starving crow in winter; and on my fingers and toes there were great curving claws, so that I looked like nothing that was known, like nothing that was animal or divine. And I sat by the pool weeping my loneliness and wildness and my stern old age; and I could do no more than cry and lament between the earth and the sky, while the beasts that tracked me listened from behind the trees, or crouched among bushes to stare at me from their drowsy covert.

"A storm arose, and when I looked again from my tall cliff I saw that great fleet rolling as in a giant's hand. At times they were pitched against the sky and staggered aloft, spinning gustily there like wind-blown leaves. Then they were hurled from these dizzy tops to the flat, moaning gulf, to the glassy, inky horror that swirled and whirled between ten waves. At times a wave leaped howling under a ship, and with a buffet dashed it into air, and chased it upwards with thunder stroke on stroke, and followed again, close as a chasing wolf, trying with hammering on hammering to beat in the wide-wombed bottom and suck out the frightened lives through one black gape. A wave fell on a ship and sunk it down with a thrust, stern as though a whole sky had tumbled at it, and the barque did not cease to go down until it crashed and sank in the sand at the bottom of the sea.

"The night came, and with it a thousand darknesses fell from the screeching sky. Not a round-eyed creature of the night might pierce an inch of that multiplied gloom. Not a creature dared creep or stand. For a great wind strode the world lashing its league-long whips in cracks of thunder, and singing to itself, now in a world-wide yell, now in an ear-dizzying hum and buzz; or with a long snarl and whine it hovered over the world searching for life to destroy.

"And at times, from the moaning and yelping blackness of the sea, there came a sound—thin-drawn as from millions of miles away, distinct as though uttered in the ear like a whisper of confidence—and I knew that a drowning man was calling on his God as he thrashed and was battered into silence, and that a blue-lipped woman was calling on her man as her hair whipped round her brows and she whirled about like a top.

"Around me the trees were dragged from earth with dying groans; they leaped into the air and flew like birds. Great waves whizzed from the sea: spinning across the cliffs and hurtling to the earth in monstrous clots of foam; the very rocks came trundling and sidling and grinding among the trees; and in that rage, and in that horror of blackness I fell asleep, or I was beaten into slumber."

Chapter 6

There I dreamed, and I saw myself changing into a stag in dream, and I felt in dream the beating of a new heart within me, and in dream I arched my neck and braced my powerful limbs.

"I awoke from the dream, and I was that which I had dreamed.

"I stood a while stamping upon a rock, with my bristling head swung high, breathing through wide nostrils all the savour of the world. For I had come marvellously from decrepitude to strength. I had writhed from the bonds of age and was young again. I smelled the turf and knew for the first time how sweet that smelled. And like lightning my moving nose sniffed all things to my heart and separated them into knowledge.

"Long I stood there, ringing my iron hoof on stone, and learning all things through my nose. Each breeze that came from the right hand or the left brought me a tale. A wind carried me the tang of wolf, and against that smell I stared and stamped. And on a wind there came the scent of my own kind, and at that I belled. Oh, loud and clear and sweet was the voice of the great stag. With what ease my lovely note went lilting. With what joy I heard the answering call. With what delight I bounded, bounded, bounded; light as a bird's plume, powerful as a storm, untiring as the sea.

"Here now was ease in ten-yard springings, with a swinging head, with the rise and fall of a swallow, with the curve and flow and urge of an otter of the sea. What a tingle dwelt about my heart! What a thrill spun to the lofty points of my antlers! How the world was new! How the sun was new! How the wind caressed me!

"With unswerving forehead and steady eye I met all that came. The old, lone wolf leaped sideways, snarling, and slunk away. The lumbering bear swung his head of hesitations and thought again; he trotted his small red eye away with him to a near-by brake. The stags of my race fled from my rocky forehead, or were pushed back and back until their legs broke under them and I trampled them to death. I was the beloved, the well known, the leader of the herds of Ireland.

"And at times I came back from my boundings about Eirè, for the strings of my heart were drawn to Ulster; and, standing away, my wide nose took the air, while I knew with joy, with terror, that men were blown on the wind. A proud head hung to the turf then, and the tears of memory rolled from a large, bright eye.

"At times I drew near, delicately, standing among thick leaves or crouched in long grown grasses, and I stared and mourned as I looked on men. For Nemed and four couples had been saved from that fierce storm, and I saw them increase and multiply until four thousand couples lived and laughed and were riotous in the sun, for the people of Nemed had small minds but great activity. They were savage fighters and hunters.

"But one time I came, drawn by that intolerable anguish of memory, and all of these people were gone: the place that knew them was silent: in the land where they had moved there was nothing of them but their bones that glinted in the sun.

"Old age came on me there. Among these bones weariness crept into my limbs. My head grew heavy, my eyes dim, my knees jerked and trembled, and there the wolves dared chase me.

"I went again to the cave that had been my home when I was an old man.

"One day I stole from the cave to snatch a mouthful of grass, for I was closely besieged by wolves. They made their rush, and I barely escaped from them. They sat beyond the cave staring at me.

"I knew their tongue. I knew all that they said to each other, and all that they said to me. But there was yet a thud left in my forehead, a deadly trample in my hoof. They did not dare come into the cave.

" 'To-morrow,' they said, 'we will tear out your throat, and gnaw on your living haunch.' "

Chapter 7

Then my soul rose to the height of Doom, and I intended all that might happen to me, and agreed to it.

" 'To-morrow,' I said, 'I will go out among ye, and I will die,' and at that the wolves howled joyfully, hungrily, impatiently.

"I slept, and I saw myself changing into a boar in dream, and I felt in dream the beating of a new heart within me, and in dream I stretched my powerful neck and braced my eager limbs. I awoke from my dream, and I was that which I had dreamed.

"The night wore away, the darkness lifted, the day came; and from without the cave the wolves called to me: " 'Come out, O Skinny Stag. Come out and die.'

"And I, with joyful heart, thrust a black bristle through the hole of the cave, and when they saw that wriggling snout, those curving tusks, that red fierce eye, the wolves fled yelping, tumbling over each other, frantic with terror; and I behind them, a wild cat for leaping, a giant for strength, a devil for ferocity; a madness and gladness of lusty, unsparing life; a killer, a champion, a boar who could not be defied.

"I took the lordship of the boars of Ireland.

"Wherever I looked among my tribes I saw love and obedience: whenever I appeared among the strangers they fled away. And the wolves feared me then, and the great, grim bear went bounding on heavy paws. I charged him at the head of my troop and rolled him over and over; but it is not easy to kill the bear, so deeply is his life packed under that stinking pelt. He picked himself up and ran, and was knocked down, and ran again blindly, butting into trees and stones. Not a claw did the big bear flash, not a tooth did he show, as he ran whimpering like a baby, or as he stood with my nose rammed against his mouth, snarling up into his nostrils.

"I challenged all that moved. All creatures but one. For men had again come to Ireland. Semion, the son of Stariath, with his people, from whom the men of Domnann and the Fir Bolg and the Galiuin are descended. These I did not chase, and when they chased me I fled.

"Often I would go, drawn by my memoried heart, to look at them as they moved among their fields; and I spoke to my mind in bitterness: When the people of Partholon were gathered in counsel my voice was heard; it was sweet to all who heard it, and the words I spoke were wise. The eyes of women brightened and softened when they looked at me. They loved to hear him when he sang who now wanders in the forest with a tusky herd."

Chapter 8

Old age again overtook me. Weariness stole into my limbs, and anguish dozed into my mind. I went to my Ulster cave and dreamed my dream, and I changed into a hawk.

"I left the ground. The sweet air was my kingdom, and my bright eye stared on a hundred miles. I soared, I swooped; I hung, motionless as a living stone, over the abyss; I lived in joy and slept in peace, and had my fill of the sweetness of life.

"During that time Beothach, the son of Iarbonel the Prophet, came to Ireland with his people, and there was a great battle between his men and the children of Semion. Long I hung over that combat, seeing every spear that hurtled, every stone that whizzed from a sling, every sword that flashed up and down, and the endless glittering of the shields. And at the end I saw that the victory was with Iarbonel. And from his people the Tuatha Dè and the Andè came, although their origin is forgotten, and learned people, because of their excellent wisdom and intelligence, say that they came from heaven.

"These are the people of Faery. All these are the gods.

"For long, long years I was a hawk. I knew every hill and stream; every field and glen of Ireland. I knew the shape of cliffs and coasts, and how all places looked under the sun or moon. And I was still a hawk when the sons of Mil drove the Tuatha Dè Danann under the ground, and held Ireland against arms or wizardry; and this was the coming of men and the beginning of genealogies.

"Then I grew old, and in my Ulster cave close to the sea I dreamed my dream, and in it I became a salmon. The green tides of ocean rose over me and my dream, so that I drowned in the sea and did not die, for I awoke in deep waters, and I was that which I dreamed.

"I had been a man, a stag, a boar, a bird, and now I was a fish. In all my changes I had joy and fulness of life. But in the water joy lay deeper, life pulsed deeper. For on land or air there is always something excessive and hindering; as arms that swing at the sides of a man, and which the mind must remember. The stag has legs to be tucked away for sleep, and untucked for movement; and the bird has wings that must be folded and pecked and cared for. But the fish has but one piece from his nose to his tail. He is complete, single and unencumbered. He turns in one turn, and goes up and down and round in one sole movement.

"How I flew through the soft element: how I joyed in the country where there is no harshness: in the element which upholds and gives way; which caresses and lets go, and will not let you fall. For man may stumble in a furrow; the stag tumble from a cliff; the hawk, wing-weary and beaten, with darkness around him and the storm behind, may dash his brains against a tree. But the home of the salmon is his delight, and the sea guards all her creatures."

Chapter 9

I became the king of the salmon, and, with my multitudes, I ranged on the tides of the world. Green and purple distances were under me: green and gold the sunlit regions above. In these latitudes I moved through a world of amber, myself amber and gold; in those others, in a sparkle of lucent blue, I curved, lit like a living jewel: and in these again, through dusks of ebony all mazed with silver, I shot and shone, the wonder of the sea.

"I saw the monsters of the uttermost ocean go heaving by; and the long lithe brutes that are toothed to their tails: and below, where gloom dipped down on gloom, vast, livid tangles that coiled and uncoiled, and lapsed down steeps and hells of the sea where even the salmon could not go.

"I knew the sea. I knew the secret caves where ocean roars to ocean; the floods that are icy cold, from which the nose of a salmon leaps back as at a sting; and the warm streams in which we rocked and dozed and were carried forward without motion. I swam on the outermost rim of the great world, where nothing was but the sea and the sky and the salmon; where even the wind was silent, and the water was clear as clean grey rock.

"And then, far away in the sea, I remembered Ulster, and there came on me an instant, uncontrollable anguish to be there. I turned, and through days and nights I swam tirelessly, jubilantly; with terror wakening in me, too, and a whisper through my being that I must reach Ireland or die.

"I fought my way to Ulster from the sea.

"Ah, how that end of the journey was hard! A sickness was racking in every one of my bones, a languor and weariness creeping through my every fibre and muscle. The waves held me back and held me back; the soft waters seemed to have grown hard; and it was as though I were urging through a rock as I strained towards Ulster from the sea.

"So tired I was! I could have loosened my frame and been swept away; I could have slept and been drifted and wafted away; swinging on grey-green billows that had turned from the land and were heaving and mounting and surging to the far blue water.

"Only the unconquerable heart of the salmon could brave that end of toil. The sound of the rivers of Ireland racing down to the sea came to me in the last numb effort: the love of Ireland bore me up: the gods of the rivers trod to me in the white-curled breakers, so that I left the sea at long, long last; and I lay in sweet water in the curve of a crannied rock, exhausted, three parts dead, triumphant."

Chapter 10

Delight and strength came to me again, and now I explored all the inland ways, the great lakes of Ireland, and her swift brown rivers.

"What a joy to lie under an inch of water basking in the sun, or beneath a shady ledge to watch the small creatures that speed like lightning on the rippling top. I saw the dragonflies flash and dart and turn, with a poise, with a speed that no other winged thing knows: I saw the hawk hover and stare and swoop: he fell like a falling stone, but he could not catch the king of the salmon: I saw the cold-eyed cat stretching along a bough level with the water, eager to hook and lift the creatures of the river. And I saw men.

"They saw me also. They came to know me and look for me. They lay in wait at the waterfalls up which I leaped like a silver flash. They held out nets for me; they hid traps under leaves; they made cords of the colour of water, of the colour of weeds—but this salmon had a nose that knew how a weed felt and how a string—they drifted meat on a sightless string, but I knew of the hook; they thrust spears at me, and threw lances which they drew back again with a cord.

"Many a wound I got from men, many a sorrowful scar.

"Every beast pursued me in the waters and along the banks; the barking, black-skinned otter came after me in lust and gust and swirl; the wild cat fished for me; the hawk and the steep-winged, spear-beaked birds dived down on me, and men crept on me with nets the width of a river, so that I got no rest. My life became a ceaseless scurry and wound and escape, a burden and anguish of watchfulness—and then I was caught."

*"My life became a ceaseless scurry and wound and escape,
a burden and anguish of watchfulness"*

Chapter 11

The fisherman of Cairill, the King of Ulster, took me in his net. Ah, that was a happy man when he saw me! He shouted for joy when he saw the great salmon in his net.

"I was still in the water as he hauled delicately. I was still in the water as he pulled me to the bank. My nose touched air and spun from it as from fire, and I dived with all my might against the bottom of the net, holding yet to the water, loving it, mad with terror that I must quit that loveliness. But the net held and I came up.

" 'Be quiet, King of the River,' said the fisherman, 'give in to Doom,' said he.

"I was in air, and it was as though I were in fire. The air pressed on me like a fiery mountain. It beat on my scales and scorched them. It rushed down my throat and scalded me. It weighed on me and squeezed me, so that my eyes felt as though they must burst from my head, my head as though it would leap from my body, and my body as though it would swell and expand and fly in a thousand pieces.

"The light blinded me, the heat tormented me, the dry air made me shrivel and gasp; and, as he lay on the grass, the great salmon whirled his desperate nose once more to the river, and leaped, leaped, leaped, even under the mountain of air. He could leap upwards, but not forwards, and yet he leaped, for in each rise he could see the twinkling waves, the rippling and curling waters.

" 'Be at ease, O King,' said the fisherman. 'Be at rest, my beloved. Let go the stream. Let the oozy marge be forgotten, and the sandy bed where the shades dance all in green and gloom, and the brown flood sings along.'

"And as he carried me to the palace he sang a song of the river, and a song of Doom, and a song in praise of the King of the Waters.

"When the king's wife saw me she desired me. I was put over a fire and roasted, and she ate me. And when time passed she gave birth to me, and I was her son and the son of Cairill the king. I remember warmth and darkness and movement and unseen sounds. All that happened I remember, from the time I was on the gridiron until the time I was born. I forget nothing of these things."

"And now," said Finnian, "you will be born again, for I shall baptize you into the family of the Living God."

* * * *

So far the story of Tuan, the son of Cairill.

No man knows if he died in those distant ages when Finnian was Abbot of Moville, or if he still keeps his fort in Ulster, watching all things, and remembering them for the glory of God and the honour of Ireland.

The Boyhood of Fionn

He was a king, a seer and a poet. He was a lord with a manifold and great train. He was our magician, our knowledgable one, our soothsayer. All that he did was sweet with him. And, however ye deem my testimony of Fionn excessive, and, although ye hold my praising overstrained, nevertheless, and by the King that is above me, he was three times better than all I say.

—Saint Patrick

Chapter 1

Fionn[1] got his first training among women. There is no wonder in that, for it is the pup's mother teaches it to fight, and women know that fighting is a necessary art although men pretend there are others that are better. These were the women druids, Bovmall and Lia Luachra.

It will be wondered why his own mother did not train him in the first natural savageries of existence, but she could not do it. She could not keep him with her for dread of the clann-Morna. The sons of Morna had been fighting and intriguing for a long time to oust her husband, Uail, from the captaincy of the Fianna of Ireland, and they had ousted him at

[1] Pronounce Fewn to rhyme with "tune."

last by killing him. It was the only way they could get rid of such a man; but it was not an easy way, for what Fionn's father did not know in arms could not be taught to him even by Morna. Still, the hound that can wait will catch a hare at last, and even Mananánn sleeps.

Fionn's mother was beautiful, long-haired Muirne: so she is always referred to. She was the daughter of Teigue, the son of Nuada from Faery, and her mother was Ethlinn. That is, her brother was Lugh of the Long Hand himself, and with a god, and such a god, for brother we may marvel that she could have been in dread of Morna or his sons, or of any one. But women have strange loves, strange fears, and these are so bound up with one another that the thing which is presented to us is not often the thing that is to be seen.

However it may be, when Uail died Muirne got married again to the King of Kerry. She gave the child to Bovmall and Lia Luachra to rear, and we may be sure that she gave injunctions with him, and many of them. The youngster was brought to the woods of Slieve Bloom and was nursed there in secret.

It is likely the women were fond of him, for other than Fionn there was no life about them. He would be their life; and their eyes may have seemed as twin benedictions resting on the small fair head. He was fair-haired, and it was for his fairness that he was afterwards called Fionn; but at this period he was known as Deimne. They saw the food they put into his little frame reproduce itself length-ways and sideways in tough inches, and in springs and energies that crawled at first, and then toddled, and then ran. He had birds for playmates, but all the creatures that live in a wood must have been his comrades. There would have been for little Fionn long hours of lonely sunshine, when the world seemed just sunshine and a sky. There would have been hours as long, when existence passed like a shade among shadows, in the multitudinous tappings of rain that dripped from leaf to leaf in the wood, and slipped so to the ground. He would have known little snaky paths, narrow enough to be filled by his own small feet, or a goat's; and he would have wondered where they went, and have marvelled again to find that, wherever they went, they came at last, through loops and twists of the branchy wood, to his own door. He may have thought of his own door as the beginning and end of the world, whence all things went, and whither all things came.

Perhaps he did not see the lark for a long time, but he would have heard him, far out of sight in the endless sky, thrilling and thrilling until the world seemed to have no other sound but that clear sweetness; and what a world it was to make that sound! Whistles and chirps, coos and caws and croaks, would have grown familiar to him. And he could at last have told which brother of the great brotherhood was making the noise he heard at any moment. The wind too: he would have listened to its thousand voices as it moved in all seasons and in all moods. Perhaps a horse would stray into the thick screen about his home, and would look as solemnly on Fionn as Fionn did on it. Or, coming suddenly on him, the horse might stare, all a-cock with eyes and ears and nose, one long-drawn facial extension, ere he turned and bounded away with manes all over him and hoofs all under him and tails all round him. A solemn-nosed, stern-eyed cow would amble and stamp in his wood to find a flyless shadow; or a strayed sheep would poke its gentle muzzle through leaves.

"A boy," he might think, as he stared on a staring horse, "a boy cannot wag his tail to keep the flies off," and that lack may have saddened him. He may have thought that a cow can snort and be dignified at the one moment, and that timidity is comely in a sheep. He would have scolded the jackdaw, and tried to out-whistle the throstle, and wondered why his pipe got tired when the blackbird's didn't.

There would be flies to be watched, slender atoms in yellow gauze that flew, and filmy specks that flittered, and sturdy, thick-ribbed brutes that pounced like cats and bit like dogs and flew like lightning. He may have mourned for the spider in bad luck who caught that fly.

There would be much to see and remember and compare, and there would be, always, his two guardians. The flies change from second to second; one cannot tell if this bird is a visitor or an inhabitant, and a sheep is just sister to a sheep; but the women were as rooted as the house itself.

Chapter 2

Were his nurses comely or harsh-looking? Fionn would not know. This was the one who picked him up when he fell, and

He might think, as he stared on a staring horse,
"a boy cannot wag his tail to keep the flies off"

that was the one who patted the bruise. This one said: "Mind you do not tumble in the well!"

And that one: "Mind the little knees among the nettles."

But he did tumble and record that the only notable thing about a well is that it is wet. And as for nettles, if they hit him he hit back. He slashed into them with a stick and brought them low. There was nothing in wells or nettles, only women dreaded them. One patronised women and instructed them and comforted them, for they were afraid about one.

They thought that one should not climb a tree!

"Next week," they said at last, "you may climb this one," and "next week" lived at the end of the world!

But the tree that was climbed was not worth while when it had been climbed twice. There was a bigger one near by. There were trees that no one could climb, with vast shadow on one side and vaster sunshine on the other. It took a long time to walk round them, and you could not see their tops.

It was pleasant to stand on a branch that swayed and sprung, and it was good to stare at an impenetrable roof of leaves and then climb into it. How wonderful the loneliness was up there! When he looked down there was an undulating floor of leaves, green and green and greener to a very blackness of greeniness; and when he looked up there were leaves again, green and less green and not green at all, up to a very snow and blindness of greeniness; and above and below and around there was sway and motion, the whisper of leaf on leaf, and the eternal silence to which one listened and at which one tried to look.

When he was six years of age his mother, beautiful, long-haired Muirne, came to see him. She came secretly, for she feared the sons of Morna, and she had paced through lonely places in many counties before she reached the hut in the wood, and the cot where he lay with his fists shut and sleep gripped in them.

He awakened to be sure. He would have one ear that would catch an unusual voice, one eye that would open, however sleepy the other one was. She took him in her arms and kissed him, and she sang a sleepy song until the small boy slept again.

We may be sure that the eye that could stay open stayed open that night as long as it could, and that the one ear listened to the sleepy song until the song got too low to be heard, until it was too tender to be felt vibrating along those soft arms, until Fionn was asleep again, with a new picture in his little head and a new notion to ponder on.

The mother of himself! His own mother!

But when he awakened she was gone.

She was going back secretly, in dread of the sons of Morna, slipping through gloomy woods, keeping away from habitations, getting by desolate and lonely ways to her lord in Kerry.

Perhaps it was he that was afraid of the sons of Morna, and perhaps she loved him.

Chapter 3

The women druids, his guardians, belonged to his father's people. Bovmall was Uail's sister, and, consequently, Fionn's aunt. Only such a blood-tie could have bound them to the clann-Baiscne, for it is not easy, having moved in the world of court and camp, to go hide with a baby in a wood; and to live, as they must have lived, in terror.

What stories they would have told the child of the sons of Morna. Of Morna himself, the huge-shouldered, stern-eyed, violent Connachtman; and of his sons—young Goll Mor mac Morna in particular, as huge-shouldered as his father, as fierce in the onset, but merry-eyed when the other was grim, and bubbling with a laughter that made men forgive even his butcheries. Of Conán Mael mac Morna his brother, gruff as a badger, bearded like a boar, bald as a crow, and with a tongue that could manage an insult where another man would not find even a stammer. His boast was that when he saw an open door he went into it, and when he saw a closed door he went into it. When he saw a peaceful man he insulted him, and when he met a man who was not peaceful he insulted him. There was Garra Duv mac Morna, and savage Art Og, who cared as little for their own skins as they did for the next man's, and Garra must have been rough indeed to have earned in that clan the name of the Rough mac Morna. There were others: wild Connachtmen all, as untameable, as unaccountable as their own wonderful countryside.

Fionn would have heard much of them, and it is likely that he practised on a nettle at taking the head off Goll, and that he hunted a sheep from cover in the implacable manner he intended later on for Conán the Swearer.

But it is of Uail mac Baiscne he would have heard most. With what a dilation of spirit the ladies would have told tales of him, Fionn's father. How their voices would have become a chant as feat was added to feat, glory piled on glory. The most famous of men and the most beautiful; the hardest fighter; the easiest giver; the kingly champion; the chief of the Fianna na h-Eirinn. Tales of how he had been way-laid and got free; of how he had been generous and got free; of how he had been angry and went marching with the speed of an eagle and the direct onfall of a storm; while in front and at the sides, angled from the prow of his terrific advance, were fleeing multitudes who did not dare to wait and scarce had time to run. And of how at last, when the time came to quell him, nothing less than the whole might of Ireland was sufficient for that great downfall.

We may be sure that on these adventures Fionn was with his father, going step for step with the long-striding hero, and heartening him mightily.

Chapter 4

He was given good training by the women in running and leaping and swimming.

One of them would take a thorn switch in her hand, and Fionn would take a thorn switch in his hand, and each would try to strike the other running round a tree.

You had to go fast to keep away from the switch behind, and a small boy feels a switch. Fionn would run his best to get away from that prickly stinger, but how he would run when it was his turn to deal the strokes!

With reason too, for his nurses had suddenly grown implacable. They pursued him with a savagery which he could not distinguish from hatred, and they swished him well whenever they got the chance.

Fionn learned to run. After a while he could buzz around a tree like a maddened fly, and oh, the joy, when he felt himself drawing from the switch and gaining from behind on its bearer! How he strained and panted to catch on that pursuing person and pursue her and get his own switch into action.

He learned to jump by chasing hares in a bumpy field. Up went the hare and up went Fionn, and away with the two of them, hopping and popping across the field. If the hare turned while Fionn was after her it was switch for Fionn; so that in a while it did not matter to Fionn which way the hare jumped for he could jump that way too. Long-ways, sideways or baw-ways, Fionn hopped where the hare hopped, and at last he was the owner of a hop that any hare would give an ear for.

He was taught to swim, and it may be that his heart sank when he fronted the lesson. The water was cold. It was deep. One could see the bottom, leagues below, millions of miles below. A small boy might shiver as he stared into that wink and blink and twink of brown pebbles and murder. And these implacable women threw him in!

How he strained and panted to catch on that pursuing person and pursue her and get his own switch into action

Perhaps he would not go in at first. He may have smiled at them, and coaxed, and hung back. It was a leg and an arm gripped then; a swing for Fionn, and out and away with him; plop and flop for him; down into chill deep death for him, and up with a splutter; with a sob; with a grasp at everything that caught nothing; with a wild flurry; with a raging despair; with a bubble and snort as he was hauled again down, and down, and down, and found as suddenly that he had been hauled out.

Fionn learned to swim until he could pop into the water like an otter and slide through it like an eel.

He used to try to chase a fish the way he chased hares in the bumpy field—but there are terrible spurts in a fish. It may be that a fish cannot hop, but he gets there in a flash, and he isn't there in another. Up or down, sideways or endways, it is all one to a fish. He goes and is gone. He twists this way and disappears the other way. He is over you when he ought to be under you, and he is biting your toe when you thought you were biting his tail.

You cannot catch a fish by swimming, but you can try, and Fionn tried. He got a grudging commendation from the terrible women when he was able to slip noiselessly in the tide, swim under water to where a wild duck was floating and grip it by the leg.

"Qu—," said the duck, and he disappeared before he had time to get the "-ack" out of him.

So the time went, and Fionn grew long and straight and tough like a sapling; limber as a willow, and with the flirt and spring of a young bird. One of the ladies may have said, "He is shaping very well, my dear," and the other replied, as is the morose privilege of an aunt, "He will never be as good as his father," but their hearts must have overflowed in the night, in the silence, in the darkness, when they thought of the living swiftness they had fashioned, and that dear fair head.

Chapter 5

One day his guardians were agitated: they held confabulations at which Fionn was not permitted to assist. A man who passed by in the morning had spoken to them. They fed the man, and during his feeding Fionn had been shooed from the door as if he were a chicken. When the stranger took his road the women went with him a short distance. As they passed the man lifted a hand and bent a knee to Fionn.

"My soul to you, young master," he said, and as he said it, Fionn knew that he could have the man's soul, or his boots, or his feet, or anything that belonged to him.

When the women returned they were mysterious and whispery. They chased Fionn into the house, and when they got him in they chased him out again. They chased each other around the house for another whisper. They calculated things by the shape of clouds, by lengths of shadows, by the flight of birds, by two flies racing on a flat stone, by throwing bones over their left shoulders, and by every kind of trick and game and chance that you could put a mind to.

They told Fionn he must sleep in a tree that night, and they put him under bonds not to sing or whistle or cough or sneeze until the morning.

Fionn did sneeze. He never sneezed so much in his life. He sat up in his tree and nearly sneezed himself out of it. Flies got up his nose, two at a time, one up each nose, and his head nearly fell off the way he sneezed.

"You are doing that on purpose," said a savage whisper from the foot of the tree.

But Fionn was not doing it on purpose. He tucked himself into a fork the way he had been taught, and he passed the crawliest, tickliest night he had ever known. After a while he did not want to sneeze, he wanted to scream: and in particular he wanted to come down from the tree. But he did not scream, nor did he leave the tree. His word was passed, and he stayed in his tree as silent as a mouse and as watchful, until he fell out of it.

In the morning a band of travelling poets were passing, and the women handed Fionn over to them. This time they could not prevent him overhearing.

"The sons of Morna!" they said.

And Fionn's heart might have swelled with rage, but that it was already swollen with adventure. And also the expected was happening. Behind every hour of their day and every moment of their lives lay the sons of Morna. Fionn had run after them as deer: he jumped after them as hares: he dived after them as fish. They lived in the house with him: they sat at the table and ate his meat. One dreamed of them, and they were expected in the morning as the sun is. They knew only too well that the son of Uail was living, and they knew that their own sons would know no ease while that son lived; for they believed in those days that like breeds like, and that the son of Uail would be Uail with additions.

His guardians knew that their hiding-place must at last be discovered, and that, when it was found, the sons of Morna would come. They had no doubt of that, and every action of their lives was based on that certainty. For no secret can remain secret. Some broken soldier tramping home to his people will find it out; a herd seeking his strayed cattle or a band of travelling musicians will get the wind of it. How many people will move through even the remotest wood in a year! The crows will tell a secret if no one else does; and under a bush, behind a clump of bracken, what eyes may there not be! But if your secret is legged like a young goat! If it is tongued like a wolf! One can hide a baby, but you cannot hide a boy. He will rove unless you tie him to a post, and he will whistle then.

The sons of Morna came, but there were only two grim women living in a lonely hut to greet them. We may be sure they were well greeted. One can imagine Goll's merry stare taking in all that could be seen; Conán's grim eye raking the women's faces while his tongue raked them again;

the Rough mac Morna shouldering here and there in the house and about it, with maybe a hatchet in his hand, and Art Og coursing further afield and vowing that if the cub was there he would find him.

Chapter 6

But Fionn was gone. He was away, bound with his band of poets for the Galtees.

It is likely they were junior poets come to the end of a year's training, and returning to their own province to see again the people at home, and to be wondered at and exclaimed at as they exhibited bits of the knowledge which they had brought from the great schools. They would know tags of rhyme and tricks about learning which Fionn would hear of; and now and again, as they rested in a glade or by the brink of a river, they might try their lessons over. They might even refer to the ogham wands on which the first words of their tasks and the opening lines of poems were cut; and it is likely that, being new to these things, they would talk of them to a youngster, and, thinking that his wits could be no better than their own, they might have explained to him how ogham was written. But it is far more likely that his women guardians had already started him at those lessons.

Still this band of young bards would have been of infinite interest to Fionn, not on account of what they had learned, but because of what they knew. All the things that he should have known as by nature: the look, the movement, the feeling of crowds; the shouldering and intercourse of man with man; the clustering of houses and how people bore themselves in and about them; the movement of armed men, and the homecoming look of wounds; tales of births, and marriages, and deaths; the chase with its multitudes of men and dogs; all the noise, the dust, the excitement of mere living. These, to Fionn, new come from leaves and shadows and the dipple and dapple of a wood, would have seemed wonderful; and the tales they would have told of their masters, their looks, fads, severities, sillinesses, would have been wonderful also.

That band should have chattered like a rookery.

They must have been young, for one time a Leinsterman came on them, a great robber named Fiacuil mac Cona, and he killed the poets. He chopped them up and chopped them down. He did not leave one poeteen of them all. He put them out of the world and out of life, so that they stopped being, and no one could tell where they went or what had really happened to them; and it is a wonder indeed that one can do that to anything let alone a band. If they were not youngsters, the bold Fiacuil could not have managed them all. Or, perhaps, he too had a band, although the record does not say so; but kill them he did, and they died that way.

Fionn saw that deed, and his blood may have been cold enough as he watched the great robber coursing the poets as a wild dog rages in a flock. And when his turn came, when they were all dead, and the grim, red-handed man trod at him, Fionn may have shivered, but he would have shown his teeth and laid roundly on the monster with his hands. Perhaps he did that, and perhaps for that he was spared.

"Who are you?" roared the staring black-mouth with the red tongue squirming in it like a frisky fish.

"The son of Uail, son of Baiscne," quoth hardy Fionn.

And at that the robber ceased to be a robber, the murderer disappeared, the black-rimmed chasm packed with red fish and precipices changed to something else, and the round eyes that had been popping out of their sockets and trying to bite, changed also. There remained a laughing and crying and loving servant who wanted to tie himself into knots if that would please the son of his great captain. Fionn went home on the robber's shoulder, and the robber gave great snorts and made great jumps and behaved like a first-rate horse. For this same Fiacuil was the husband of Bovmall, Fionn's aunt. He had taken to the wilds when clann-Baiscne was broken, and he was at war with a world that had dared to kill his Chief.

Chapter 7

A new life for Fionn in the robber's den that was hidden in a vast cold marsh.

A tricky place that would be, with sudden exits and even suddener entrances, and with damp, winding, spidery places to hoard treasure in, or to hide oneself in.

If the robber was a solitary he would, for lack of someone else, have talked greatly to Fionn. He would have shown his weapons and demonstrated how he used them, and with what slash he chipped his victim, and with what slice he chopped him. He would have told why a slash was enough for this man and why that man should be sliced. All men are masters when one is young, and Fionn would have found knowledge here also. He would have seen Fiacuil's great spear that had thirty rivets of Arabian gold in its socket, and that had to be kept wrapped up and tied down so that it would not kill people out of mere spitefulness. It had come from Faery, out of the Shi' of Aillen mac Midna, and it would be brought back again later on between the same man's shoulder-blades.

What tales that man could tell a boy, and what questions a boy could ask him. He would have known a thousand tricks, and because our instinct is to teach, and because no man can keep a trick from a boy, he would show them to Fionn.

There was the marsh too; a whole new life to be learned; a complicated, mysterious, dank, slippery, reedy, treacherous life, but with its own beauty and an allurement that could grow on one, so that you could forget the solid world and love only that which quaked and gurgled.

In this place you may swim. By this sign and this you will know if it is safe to do so, said Fiacuil mac Cona; but in this place, with this sign on it and that, you must not venture a toe.

But where Fionn would venture his toes his ears would follow.

There are coiling weeds down there, the robber counselled him; there are thin, tough, snaky binders that will trip you and grip you, that will pull you and will not let you go again until you are drowned; until you are swaying and swinging away below, with outstretched arms, with outstretched legs, with a face all stares and smiles and jockeyings, gripped in those leathery arms, until there is no more to be gripped of you even by them.

"Watch these and this and that," Fionn would have been told, "and always swim with a knife in your teeth."

He lived there until his guardians found out where he was and came after him. Fiacuil gave him up to them, and he was brought home again to the woods of Slieve Bloom, but he had gathered great knowledge and new supplenesses.

The sons of Morna left him alone for a long time. Having made their essay they grew careless.

"Let him be," they said. "He will come to us when the time comes."

But it is likely too that they had had their own means of getting information about him. How he shaped? what muscles he had? and did he spring clean from the mark or had he to get off with a push?

Fionn stayed with his guardians and hunted for them. He could run a deer down and haul it home by the reluctant skull. "Come on, Goll," he would say to his stag, or, lifting it over a tussock with a tough grip on the snout, "Are you coming, bald Conàn, or shall I kick you in the neck?"

The time must have been nigh when he would think of taking the world itself by the nose, to haul it over tussocks and drag it into his pen; for he was of the breed in whom mastery is born, and who are good masters.

But reports of his prowess were getting abroad. Clann-Morna began to stretch itself uneasily, and, one day, his guardians sent him on his travels.

"It is best for you to leave us now," they said to the tall stripling, "for the sons of Morna are watching again to kill you."

The woods at that may have seemed haunted. A stone might sling at one from a tree-top; but from which tree of a thousand trees did it come? An arrow buzzing by one's ear would slide into the ground and quiver there silently, menacingly, hinting of the brothers it had left in the quiver behind; to the right? to the left? how many brothers? in how many quivers . . .? Fionn was a woodsman, but he had only two eyes to look with, one set of feet to carry him in one sole direction. But when he was looking to the front what, or how many whats, could be staring at him from the back? He might face in this direction, away from, or towards a smile on a hidden face and a finger on a string. A lance might slide at him from this bush or from the one yonder . . . In the night he might have fought them; his ears against theirs; his noiseless feet against their lurking ones; his knowledge of the wood against their legion: but during the day he had no chance.

Fionn went to seek his fortune, to match himself against all that might happen, and to carve a name for himself that will live while Time has an ear and knows an Irishman.

Chapter 8

Fionn went away, and now he was alone. But he was as fitted for loneliness as the crane is that haunts the solitudes and bleak wastes of the sea; for the man with a thought has a comrade, and Fionn's mind worked as featly as his body did. To be alone was no trouble to him who, however surrounded, was to be lonely his life long; for this will be said of Fionn when all is said, that all that came to him went from him, and that happiness was never his companion for more than a moment.

But he was not now looking for loneliness. He was seeking the instruction of a crowd, and therefore when he met a crowd he went into it. His eyes were skilled to observe in the moving dusk and dapple of green woods. They were trained to pick out of shadows birds that were themselves dun-coloured shades, and to see among trees the animals that are coloured like the bark of trees. The hare crouching in the fronds was visible to him, and the fish that swayed invisibly in the sway and flicker of a green bank. He would see all that was to be seen, and he would see all that is passed by the eye that is half blind from use and wont.

At Moy Lifé he came on lads swimming in a pool; and, as he looked on them sporting in the flush tide, he thought that the tricks they performed were not hard for him, and that he could have shown them new ones.

Boys must know what another boy can do, and they will match themselves against everything. They did their best under these observing eyes, and it was not long until he was invited to compete with them and show his mettle. Such an invitation is a challenge; it is almost, among boys, a declaration of war. But Fionn was so far beyond them in swimming that even the word master did not apply to that superiority.

While he was swimming one remarked: "He is fair and well shaped," and thereafter he was called "Fionn" or the Fair One. His name came from boys, and will, perhaps, be preserved by them.

He stayed with these lads for some time, and it may be that they idolised him at first, for it is the way with boys to be astounded and enraptured by feats; but in the end, and that was inevitable, they grew jealous of the stranger. Those who had been the champions before he came would marshal each other, and, by social pressure, would muster all the others against him; so that in the end not a friendly eye was turned on Fionn in that assembly. For not only did he beat them at swimming, he beat their best at running and jumping, and when the sport degenerated into violence, as it was bound to, the roughness of Fionn would be ten times as rough as the roughness of the roughest rough they could put forward. Bravery is pride when one is young, and Fionn was proud.

There must have been anger in his mind as he went away leaving that lake behind him, and those snarling and scowling boys, but there would have been disappointment also, for his desire at this time should have been towards friendliness.

He went thence to Lock Léin and took service with the King of Finntraigh. That kingdom may have been thus called from Fionn himself and would have been known by another name when he arrived there.

He hunted for the King of Finntraigh, and it soon grew evident that there was no hunter in his service to equal Fionn. More, there was no hunter of them all who even distantly approached him in excellence. The others ran after deer, using the speed of their legs, the noses of their dogs and a thousand well-worn tricks to bring them within reach, and, often enough, the animal escaped them. But the deer that Fionn got the track of did not get away, and it seemed even that the animals sought him, so many did he catch.

The king marvelled at the stories that were told of this new hunter, but as kings are greater than other people so they are more curious; and, being on the plane of excellence, they must see all that is excellently told of.

The king wished to see him, and Fionn must have wondered what the king thought as that gracious lord looked on him. Whatever was thought, what the king said was as direct in utterance as it was in observation.

"If Uail the son of Baiscne has a son," said the king, "you would surely be that son."

We are not told if the King of Finntraigh said anything more, but we know that Fionn left his service soon afterwards.

He went southwards and was next in the employment of the King of Kerry, the same lord who had married his own mother. In that service he came to such consideration that we hear of him as playing a match of chess with the king, and by this game we know that he was still a boy in his mind however mightily his limbs were spreading. Able as he was in sports and huntings, he was yet too young to be politic, but he remained impolitic to the end of his days, for whatever he was able to do he would do, no matter who was offended thereat; and whatever he was not able to do he would do also. That was Fionn.

Once, as they rested on a chase, a debate arose among the Fianna-Finn as to what was the finest music in the world.

"Tell us that," said Fionn turning to Oisín.[2]

"The cuckoo calling from the tree that is highest in the hedge," cried his merry son.

"A good sound," said Fionn. "And you, Oscar," he asked, "what is to your mind the finest of music?"

"The top of music is the ring of a spear on a shield," cried the stout lad.

"It is a good sound," said Fionn.

And the other champions told their delight; the belling of a stag across water, the baying of a tuneful pack heard in the distance, the song of a lark, the laugh of a gleeful girl, or the whisper of a moved one.

"They are good sounds all," said Fionn.

"Tell us, chief," one ventured, "what you think?"

"The music of what happens," said great Fionn, "that is the finest music in the world."

He loved "what happened," and would not evade it by the swerve of a hair; so on this occasion what was occurring he would have occur, although a king was his rival and his master. It may be that his mother was watching the match and that he could not but exhibit his skill before

[2] Pronounced Usheen.

her. He committed the enormity of winning seven games in succession from the king himself!!!

It is seldom indeed that a subject can beat a king at chess, and this monarch was properly amazed.

"Who are you at all?" he cried, starting back from the chessboard and staring on Fionn.

"I am the son of a countryman of the Luigne of Tara," said Fionn.

He may have blushed as he said it, for the king, possibly for the first time, was really looking at him, and was looking back through twenty years of time as he did so. The observation of a king is faultless—it is proved a thousand times over in the tales, and this king's equipment was as royal as the next.

"You are no such son," said the indignant monarch, "but you are the son that Muirne my wife bore to Uail mac Baiscne."

And at that Fionn had no more to say; but his eyes may have flown to his mother and stayed there.

"You cannot remain here," his step-father continued. "I do not want you killed under my protection," he explained, or complained.

Perhaps it was on Fionn's account he dreaded the sons of Morna, but no one knows what Fionn thought of him for he never thereafter spoke of his step-father. As for Muirne she must have loved her lord; or she may have been terrified in truth of the sons of Morna and for Fionn; but it is so also, that if a woman loves her second husband she can dislike all that reminds her of the first one.

Fionn went on his travels again.

Chapter 9

All desires save one are fleeting, but that one lasts for ever. Fionn, with all desires, had the lasting one, for he would go anywhere and forsake anything for wisdom; and it was in search of this that he went to the place where Finegas lived on a bank of the Boyne Water. But for dread of the clann-Morna he did not go as Fionn. He called himself Deimne on that journey.

We get wise by asking questions, and even if these are not answered we get wise, for a well-packed question carries its answer on its back as a snail carries its shell. Fionn asked every question he could think of, and his master, who was a poet, and so an honourable man, answered them all, not to the limit of his patience, for it was limitless, but to the limit of his ability.

"Why do you live on the bank of a river?" was one of these questions.

"Because a poem is a revelation, and it is by the brink of running water that poetry is revealed to the mind."

"How long have you been here?" was the next query.

"Seven years," the poet answered.

"It is a long time," said wondering Fionn.

"I would wait twice as long for a poem," said the inveterate bard.

"Have you caught good poems?" Fionn asked him.

"The poems I am fit for," said the mild master. "No person can get more than that, for a man's readiness is his limit."

"Would you have got as good poems by the Shannon or the Suir or by sweet Ana Lifé?"

"They are good rivers," was the answer. "They all belong to good gods."

"But why did you choose this river out of all the rivers?"

Finegas beamed on his pupil.

"I would tell you anything," said he, "and I will tell you that."

Fionn sat at the kindly man's feet, his hands absent among tall grasses, and listening with all his ears.

"A prophecy was made to me," Finegas began. "A man of knowledge foretold that I should catch the Salmon of Knowledge in the Boyne Water."

"And then?" said Fionn eagerly.

"Then I would have All Knowledge."

"And after that?" the boy insisted.

"What should there be after that?" the poet retorted.

"I mean, what would you do with All Knowledge?"

"A weighty question," said Finegas smilingly. "I could answer it if I had All Knowledge, but not until then. What would you do, my dear?"

"I would make a poem," Fionn cried.

"I think too," said the poet, "that that is what would be done."

In return for instruction Fionn had taken over the service of his master's hut, and as he went about the household duties, drawing the water, lighting the fire, and carrying rushes for the floor and the beds, he thought over all the poet had taught him, and his mind dwelt on the rules of metre, the cunningness of words, and the need for a clean, brave mind. But in his thousand thoughts he yet remembered the Salmon of Knowledge as eagerly as his master did. He already venerated Finegas for his great learning, his poetic skill, for an hundred reasons; but, looking on him as the ordained eater of the Salmon of Knowledge, he venerated him to the edge of measure. Indeed, he loved as well as venerated this master because of his unfailing kindness, his patience, his readiness to teach, and his skill in teaching.

"I have learned much from you, dear master," said Fionn gratefully.

"All that I have is yours if you can take it," the poet answered, "for you are entitled to all that you can take, but to no more than that. Take, so, with both hands."

"You may catch the salmon while I am with you," the hopeful boy mused. "Would not that be a great happening!" and he stared in ecstasy across the grass at those visions which a boy's mind knows.

"Let us pray for that," said Finegas fervently.

"Here is a question," Fionn continued. "How does this salmon get wisdom into his flesh?"

"There is a hazel bush overhanging a secret pool in a secret place. The Nuts of Knowledge drop from the Sacred Bush into the pool, and as they float, a salmon takes them in his mouth and eats them."

"It would be almost as easy," the boy submitted, "if one were to set on the track of the Sacred Hazel and eat the nuts straight from the bush."

"That would not be very easy," said the poet, "and yet it is not as easy as that, for the bush can only be found by its own knowledge, and that knowledge can only be got by eating the nuts, and the nuts can only be got by eating the salmon."

"We must wait for the salmon," said Fionn in a rage of resignation.

Chapter 10

Life continued for him in a round of timeless time, wherein days and nights were uneventful and were yet filled with interest. As the day packed its load of strength into his frame, so it added its store of knowledge to his mind, and each night sealed the twain, for it is in the night that we make secure what we have gathered in the day.

If he had told of these days he would have told of a succession of meals and sleeps, and of an endless conversation, from which his mind would now and again slip away to a solitude of its own, where, in large hazy atmospheres, it swung and drifted and reposed. Then he would be back again, and it was a pleasure for him to catch up on the thought that was forward and re-create for it all the matter he had missed. But he could not often make these sleepy sallies; his master was too experienced a teacher to allow any such bright-faced, eager-eyed abstractions, and as the druid women had switched his legs around a tree, so Finegas chased his mind, demanding sense in his questions and understanding in his replies.

To ask questions can become the laziest and wobbliest occupation of a mind, but when you must yourself answer the problem that you have posed, you will meditate your question with care and frame it with precision. Fionn's mind learned to jump in a bumpier field than that in which he had chased rabbits. And when he had asked his question, and given his own answer to it, Finegas would take the matter up and make clear to him where the query was badly formed or at what point the answer had begun to go astray, so that Fionn came to understand by what successions a good question grows at last to a good answer.

One day, not long after the conversation told of, Finegas came to the place where Fionn was. The poet had a shallow osier basket on his arm, and on his face there was a look that was at once triumphant and gloomy. He was excited certainly, but be was sad also, and as he stood gazing on Fionn his eyes were so kind that the boy was touched, and they were yet so melancholy that it almost made Fionn weep.

"What is it, my master?" said the alarmed boy.

The poet placed his osier basket on the grass.

"Look in the basket, dear son," he said.

Fionn looked.

"There is a salmon in the basket."

"It is The Salmon," said Finegas with a great sigh. Fionn leaped for delight.

"I am glad for you, master," he cried. "Indeed I am glad for you."

"And I am glad, my dear soul," the master rejoined.

But, having said it, he bent his brow to his hand and for a long time he was silent and gathered into himself.

"What should be done now?" Fionn demanded, as he stared on the beautiful fish.

Finegas rose from where he sat by the osier basket.

"I will be back in a short time," he said heavily. "While I am away you may roast the salmon, so that it will be ready against my return."

"I will roast it indeed," said Fionn.

The poet gazed long and earnestly on him.

"You will not eat any of my salmon while I am away?" he asked.

"I will not eat the littlest piece," said Fionn.

"I am sure you will not," the other murmured, as he turned and walked slowly across the grass and behind the sheltering bushes on the ridge.

Fionn cooked the salmon. It was beautiful and tempting and savoury as it smoked on a wooden platter among cool green leaves; and it looked all these to Finegas when he came from behind the fringing bushes and sat in the grass outside his door. He gazed on the fish with more than his eyes. He looked on it with his heart, with his soul in his eyes, and when he turned to look on Fionn the boy did not know whether the love that was in his eyes was for the fish or for himself. Yet he did know that a great moment had arrived for the poet.

"So," said Finegas, "you did not eat it on me after all?"

"Did I not promise?" Fionn replied.

"And yet," his master continued, "I went away so that you might eat the fish if you felt you had to."

"Why should I want another man's fish?" said proud Fionn.

"Because young people have strong desires. I thought you might have tasted it, and then you would have eaten it on me."

"I did taste it by chance," Fionn laughed, "for while the fish was roasting a great blister rose on its skin. I did not like the look of that blister, and I pressed it down with my thumb. That burned my thumb, so I popped it in my mouth to heal the smart. If your salmon tastes as nice as my thumb did," he laughed, "it will taste very nice."

"What did you say your name was, dear heart?" the poet asked.

"I said my name was Deimne."

"Your name is not Deimne," said the mild man, "your name is Fionn."

"That is true," the boy answered, "but I do not know how you know it."

"Even if I have not eaten the Salmon of Knowledge I have some small science of my own."

"It is very clever to know things as you know them," Fionn replied wonderingly. "What more do you know of me, dear master?"

"I know that I did not tell you the truth," said the heavy-hearted man.

"What did you tell me instead of it?"

"I told you a lie."

"It is not a good thing to do," Fionn admitted. "What sort of a lie was the lie, master?"

"I told you that the Salmon of Knowledge was to be caught by me, according to the prophecy."

"Yes."

"That was true indeed, and I have caught the fish. But I did not tell you that the salmon was not to be eaten by me, although that also was in the prophecy, and that omission was the lie."

"It is not a great lie," said Fionn soothingly.

"It must not become a greater one," the poet replied sternly.

"Who was the fish given to?" his companion wondered.

"It was given to you," Finegas answered. "It was given to Fionn, the son of Uail, the son of Baiscne, and it will be given to him."

"You shall have a half of the fish," cried Fionn.

"I will not eat a piece of its skin that is as small as the point of its smallest bone," said the resolute and trembling bard. "Let you now eat up the fish, and I shall watch you and give praise to the gods of the Underworld and of the Elements."

Fionn then ate the Salmon of Knowledge, and when it had disappeared a great jollity and tranquillity and exuberance returned to the poet.

"Ah," said he, "I had a great combat with that fish."

"Did it fight for its life?" Fionn inquired.

"It did, but that was not the fight I meant."

"You shall eat a Salmon of Knowledge too," Fionn assured him.

"You have eaten one," cried the blithe poet, "and if you make such a promise it will be because you know."

"I promise it and know it," said Fionn, "you shall eat a Salmon of Knowledge yet."

Chapter 11

He had received all that he could get from Finegas. His education was finished and the time had come to test it, and to try all else that he had of mind and body. He bade farewell to the gentle poet, and set out for Tara of the Kings.

It was Samhain-tide, and the feast of Tara was being held, at which all that was wise or skilful or well-born in Ireland were gathered together.

This is how Tara was when Tara was. There was the High King's palace with its fortification; without it was another fortification enclosing the four minor palaces, each of which was maintained by one of the four provincial kings; without that again was the great banqueting hall, and around it and enclosing all of the sacred hill in its gigantic bound ran the main outer ramparts of Tara. From it, the centre of Ireland, four great roads went, north, south, east, and west, and along these roads, from the top and the bottom and the two sides of Ireland, there moved for weeks before Samhain an endless stream of passengers.

Here a gay band went carrying rich treasure to decorate the pavilion of a Munster lord. On another road a vat of seasoned yew, monstrous as a house on wheels and drawn by an hundred laborious oxen, came bumping and joggling the ale that thirsty Connaught princes would drink. On a road again the learned men of Leinster, each with an idea in his head that would discomfit a northern ollav and make a southern one gape and fidget, would be marching solemnly, each by a horse that was piled high on the back and widely at the sides with clean-peeled willow or oaken wands, that were carved from the top to the bottom with the ogham signs; the first lines of poems (for it was an offence against wisdom to commit more than initial lines to writing), the names and dates of kings, the procession of laws of Tara and of the sub-kingdoms, the names of places and their meanings. On the brown stallion ambling peacefully yonder there might go the warring of the gods for two or ten thousand years; this mare with the dainty pace and the vicious eye might be sidling under a load of oaken odes in honour of her owner's family, with a few bundles of tales of wonder added in case they might be useful; and perhaps the restive piebald was backing the history of Ireland into a ditch.

On such a journey all people spoke together, for all were friends, and no person regarded the weapon in another man's hand other than as an implement to poke a reluctant cow with, or to pacify with loud wallops some hoof-proud colt.

Into this teem and profusion of jolly humanity Fionn slipped, and if his mood had been as bellicose as a wounded boar he would yet have found no man to quarrel with, and if his eye had been as sharp as a jealous husband's he would have found no eye to meet it with calculation or menace or fear; for the Peace of Ireland was in being, and for six weeks man was neighbour to man, and the nation was the guest of the High King.

Fionn went in with the notables.

His arrival had been timed for the opening day and the great feast of welcome. He may have marvelled, looking on the bright city, with its pillars of gleaming bronze and the roofs that were painted in many colours, so that each house seemed to be covered by the spreading wings of some gigantic and gorgeous bird. And the palaces themselves, mellow with red oak, polished within and without by the wear and the care of a thousand years, and carved with the patient skill of unending generations of the most famous artists of the most artistic country of the western world, would have given him much to marvel at also. It must have seemed like a city of dream, a city to catch the heart, when, coming over the great plain, Fionn saw Tara of the Kings held on its hill as in a hand to gather all the gold of the falling sun, and to restore a brightness as mellow and tender as that universal largess.

In the great banqueting hall everything was in order for the feast. The nobles of Ireland with their winsome consorts, the learned and artistic professions represented by the pick of their time were in place. The Ard-Rí, Conn of the Hundred Battles, had taken his place on the raised dais which commanded the whole of that vast hall. At his right hand his son Art, to be afterwards as famous as his famous father, took his seat, and on his left Goll mor mac Morna, chief of the Fianna of Ireland, had the seat of honour. As the High King took his place he could see every person who was noted in the land for any reason. He would know every one who was present, for the fame of all men is sealed at Tara, and behind his chair a herald stood to tell anything the king might not know or had forgotten.

Conn gave the signal and his guests seated themselves.

The time had come for the squires to take their stations behind their masters and mistresses. But, for the moment, the great room was seated, and the doors were held to allow a moment of respect to pass before the servers and squires came in.

Looking over his guests, Conn observed that a young man was yet standing.

"There is a gentleman," he murmured, "for whom no seat has been found."

We may be sure that the Master of the Banquet blushed at that.

"And," the king continued, "I do not seem to know the young man."

Nor did his herald, nor did the unfortunate Master, nor did anybody; for the eyes of all were now turned where the king's went.

"Give me my horn," said the gracious monarch.

The horn of state was put to his hand.

"Young gentleman," he called to the stranger, "I wish to drink to your health and to welcome you to Tara."

The young man came forward then, greater-shouldered than any mighty man of that gathering, longer and cleaner limbed, with his fair curls dancing about his beardless face. The king put the great horn into his hand.

"Tell me your name," he commanded gently.

"I am Fionn, the son of Uail, the son of Baiscne," said the youth.

And at that saying a touch as of lightning went through the gathering so that each person quivered, and the son of the great, murdered captain looked by the king's shoulder into the twinkling eye of Goll. But no word was uttered, no movement made except the movement and the utterance of the Ard-Rí.

"You are the son of a friend," said the great-hearted monarch. "You shall have the seat of a friend."

He placed Fionn at the right hand of his own son Art.

Chapter 12

It is to be known that on the night of the Feast of Samhain the doors separating this world and the next one are opened, and the inhabitants of either world can leave their respective spheres and appear in the world of the other beings.

Now there was a grandson to the Dagda Mor, the Lord of the Underworld, and he was named Aillen mac Midna, out of Shí Finnachy, and this Aillen bore an implacable enmity to Tara and the Ard-Rí.

As well as being monarch of Ireland her High King was chief of the people learned in magic, and it is possible that at some time Conn had adventured into Tir na n-Og, the Land of the Young, and had done some deed or misdeed in Aillen's lordship or in his family. It must have been an ill deed in truth, for it was in a very rage of revenge that Aillen came yearly at the permitted time to ravage Tara.

Nine times he had come on this mission of revenge, but it is not to be supposed that he could actually destroy the holy city: the Ard-Rí and magicians could prevent that, but he could yet do a damage so considerable that it was worth Conn's while to take special extra precautions against him, including the precaution of chance.

Therefore, when the feast was over and the banquet had commenced, the Hundred Fighter stood from his throne and looked over his assembled people.

The Chain of Silence was shaken by the attendant whose duty and honour was the Silver Chain, and at that delicate chime the hall went silent, and a general wonder ensued as to what matter the High King would submit to his people.

"Friends and heroes," said Conn, "Aillen, the son of Midna, will come to-night from Slieve Fuaid with occult, terrible fire against our city. Is there among you one who loves Tara and the king, and who will undertake our defence against that being?"

He spoke in silence, and when he had finished he listened to the same silence, but it was now deep, ominous, agonized. Each man glanced uneasily on his neighbour and then stared at his wine-cup or his fingers. The hearts of young men went hot for a gallant moment and were chilled in the succeeding one, for they had all heard of Aillen out of Shí Finnachy in the north. The lesser gentlemen looked under their brows at the greater champions, and these peered furtively at the greatest of all. Art og mac Morna of the Hard Strokes fell to biting his fingers, Conán the Swearer and Garra mac Morna grumbled irritably to each other and at their neighbours, even Caelte, the son of Ronán, looked down into his own lap, and Goll Mor sipped at his wine without any twinkle in his eye. A horrid embarrassment came into the great hall, and as the High King stood in that palpitating silence his noble face changed from kindly to grave and from that to a terrible sternness. In another moment, to the undying shame of every person present, he would have been compelled to lift his own challenge and declare himself the champion of Tara for that night, but the shame that was on the faces of his people would remain in the heart of their king. Goll's merry mind would help him to forget, but even his heart would be wrung by a memory that he would not dare to face. It was at that terrible moment that Fionn stood up.

"What," said he, "will be given to the man who undertakes this defence?"

"All that can be rightly asked will be royally bestowed," was the king's answer.

"Who are the sureties?" said Fionn.

"The kings of Ireland, and Red Cith with his magicians."

"I will undertake the defence," said Fionn. And on that, the kings and magicians who were present bound themselves to the fulfilment of the bargain.

Fionn marched from the banqueting hall, and as he went, all who were present of nobles and retainers and servants acclaimed him and wished him luck. But in their hearts they were bidding him good-bye, for all were assured that the lad was marching to a death so unescapeable that he might already be counted as a dead man.

It is likely that Fionn looked for help to the people of the Shí themselves, for, through his mother, he belonged to the tribes of Dana, although, on the father's side, his blood was well compounded with mortal clay. It may be, too, that he knew how events would turn, for he had eaten the Salmon of Knowledge. Yet it is not recorded that on this occasion he invoked any magical art as he did on other adventures.

Fionn's way of discovering whatever was happening and hidden was always the same and is many times referred to. A shallow, oblong dish of pure, pale gold was brought to him. This dish was filled with clear water. Then Fionn would bend his head and stare into the water, and as he stared he would place his thumb in his mouth under his "Tooth of Knowledge," his "wisdom tooth."

Knowledge, may it be said, is higher than magic and is more to be sought. It is quite possible to see what is happening and yet not know what is forward, for while seeing is believing it does not follow that either seeing or believing is knowing. Many a person can see a thing and believe a thing and know just as little about it as the person who does neither. But Fionn would see and know, or he would understand a decent ratio of his visions. That he was versed in magic is true, for he was ever known as the Knowledgeable man, and later he had two magicians in his household named Dirim and mac-Reith to do the rough work of knowledge for their busy master.

It was not from the Shí, however, that assistance came to Fionn.

Chapter 13

He marched through the successive fortifications until he came to the outer, great wall, the boundary of the city, and when he had passed this he was on the wide plain of Tara.

Other than himself no person was abroad, for on the night of the Feast of Samhain none but a madman would quit the shelter of a house even if it were on fire; for whatever disasters might be within a house would be as nothing to the calamities without it.

The noise of the banquet was not now audible to Fionn—it is possible, however, that there was a shamefaced silence in the great hall—and the lights of the city were hidden by the successive great ramparts. The sky was over him; the earth under him; and than these there was nothing, or there was but the darkness and the wind.

But darkness was not a thing to terrify him, bred in the nightness of a wood and the very fosterling of gloom; nor could the wind afflict his ear or his heart. There was no note in its orchestra that he had not brooded on and become, which becoming is magic. The long-drawn moan of it; the thrilling whisper and hush; the shrill, sweet whistle, so thin it can scarcely be heard, and is taken more by the nerves than by the ear; the screech, sudden as a devil's yell and loud as ten thunders; the cry as of one who flies with backward look to the shelter of leaves and darkness; and the sob as of one stricken with an age-long misery, only at times remembered, but remembered then with what a pang! His ear knew by what successions they arrived, and by what stages they grew and diminished. Listening in the dark to the bundle of noises which make a noise he could disentangle them and assign a place and a reason to each gradation of sound that formed the chorus: there was the patter of a rabbit, and there the scurrying of a hare; a bush rustled yonder, but that brief rustle was a bird; that pressure was a wolf, and this hesitation a fox; the scraping yonder was but a rough leaf against bark, and the scratching beyond it was a ferret's claw.

Fear cannot be where knowledge is, and Fionn was not fearful.

His mind, quietly busy on all sides, picked up one sound and dwelt on it. "A man," said Fionn, and he listened in that direction, back towards the city.

A man it was, almost as skilled in darkness as Fionn himself.

"This is no enemy," Fionn thought; "his walking is open."

"Who comes?" he called.

"A friend," said the newcomer.

"Give a friend's name," said Fionn.

"Fiacuil mac Cona," was the answer.

"Ah, my pulse and heart!" cried Fionn, and he strode a few paces to meet the great robber who had fostered him among the marshes.

"So you are not afraid," he said joyfully.

"I am afraid in good truth," Fiacuil whispered, "and the minute my business with you is finished I will trot back as quick as legs will carry me. May the gods protect my going as they protected my coming," said the robber piously.

"Amen," said Fionn, "and now, tell me what you have come for?"

"Have you any plan against this lord of the Shí?" Fiacuil whispered.

"I will attack him," said Fionn.

"That is not a plan," the other groaned, "we do not plan to deliver an attack but to win a victory."

"Is this a very terrible person?" Fionn asked.

"Terrible indeed. No one can get near him or away from him. He comes out of the Shí playing sweet, low music on a timpan and a pipe, and all who hear this music fall asleep."

"I will not fall asleep," said Fionn.

"You will indeed, for everybody does."

"What happens then?" Fionn asked.

"When all are asleep Aillen mac Midna blows a dart of fire out of his mouth, and everything that is touched by that fire is destroyed, and he can blow his fire to an incredible distance and to any direction."

"You are very brave to come to help me," Fionn murmured, "especially when you are not able to help me at all."

"I can help," Fiacuil replied, "but I must be paid."

"What payment?"

"A third of all you earn and a seat at your council."

"I grant that," said Fionn, "and now, tell me your plan?"

"You remember my spear with the thirty rivets of Arabian gold in its socket?"

"The one," Fionn queried, "that had its head wrapped in a blanket and was stuck in a bucket of water and was chained to a wall as well—the venomous Birgha?"

"That one," Fiacuil replied.

"It is Aillen mac Midna's own spear," he continued, "and it was taken out of his Shí by your father."

"Well?" said Fionn, wondering nevertheless where Fiacuil got the spear, but too generous to ask.

"When you hear the great man of the Shí coming, take the wrappings off the head of the spear and bend your face over it; the heat of the spear, the stench of it, all its pernicious and acrid qualities will prevent you from going to sleep."

"Are you sure of that?" said Fionn.

"You couldn't go to sleep close to that stench; nobody could," Fiacuil replied decidedly.

He continued: "Aillen mac Midna will be off his guard when he stops playing and begins to blow his fire; he will think everybody is asleep; then you can deliver the attack you were speaking of, and all good luck go with it."

"I will give him back his spear," said Fionn.

"Here it is," said Fiacuil, taking the Birgha from under his cloak. "But be as careful of it, my pulse, be as frightened of it as you are of the man of Dana."

"I will be frightened of nothing," said Fionn, "and the only person I will be sorry for is that Aillen mac Midna, who is going to get his own spear back."

"I will go away now," his companion whispered, "for it is growing darker where you would have thought there was no more room for darkness, and there is an eerie feeling abroad which I do not like. That man from the Shí may come any minute, and if I catch one sound of his music I am done for."

The robber went away and again Fionn was alone.

Chapter 14

He listened to the retreating footsteps until they could be heard no more, and the one sound that came to his tense ears was the beating of his own heart.

Even the wind had ceased, and there seemed to be nothing in the world but the darkness and himself. In that gigantic blackness, in that unseen quietude and vacancy, the mind could cease to be personal to itself. It could be overwhelmed and merged in space, so that consciousness would be transferred or dissipated, and one might sleep standing; for the mind fears loneliness more than all else, and will escape to the moon rather than be driven inwards on its own being.

But Fionn was not lonely, and he was not afraid when the son of Midna came.

A long stretch of the silent night had gone by, minute following minute in a slow sequence, wherein as there was no change there was no time; wherein there was no past and no future, but a stupefying, endless present which is almost the annihilation of consciousness. A change came then, for the clouds had also been moving and the moon at last was sensed behind them—not as a radiance, but as a percolation of light, a gleam that was strained through matter after matter and was less than the very wraith or remembrance of itself; a thing seen so narrowly, so sparsely, that the eye could doubt if it was or was not seeing, and might conceive that its own memory was re-creating that which was still absent.

But Fionn's eye was the eye of a wild creature that spies on darkness and moves there wittingly. He saw, then, not a thing but a movement; something that was darker than the darkness it loomed on; not a being but a presence, an, as it were, impending pressure. And in a little he heard the deliberate pace of that great being.

Fionn bent to his spear and unloosed its coverings.

Then from the darkness there came another sound; a low, sweet sound; thrillingly joyous, thrillingly low; so low the ear could scarcely note it, so sweet the ear wished to catch nothing else and would strive to hear it rather than all sounds that may be heard by man: the music of another world! the unearthly, dear melody of the Shí! So sweet it was that the sense strained to it, and having reached must follow drowsily in its wake, and would merge in it, and could not return again to its own place until that strange harmony was finished and the ear restored to freedom.

But Fionn had taken the covering from his spear, and with his brow pressed close to it he kept his mind and all his senses engaged on that sizzling, murderous point.

The music ceased and Aillen hissed a fierce blue flame from his mouth, and it was as though he hissed lightning.

Here it would seem that Fionn used magic, for spreading out his fringed mantle he caught the flame. Rather he stopped it, for it slid from the mantle and sped down into the earth to the depth of twenty-six spans; from which that slope is still called the Glen of the Mantle, and the rise on which Aillen stood is known as the Ard of Fire.

One can imagine the surprise of Aillen mac Midna, seeing his fire caught and quenched by an invisible hand. And one can imagine that at this check he might be frightened, for who would be more terrified than a magician who sees his magic fail, and who, knowing of power, will guess at powers of which he has no conception and may well dread.

Everything had been done by him as it should be done. His pipe had been played and his timpan, all who heard that music should be asleep, and yet his fire was caught in full course and was quenched.

Aillen, with all the terrific strength of which he was master, blew again, and the great jet of blue flame came roaring and whistling from him and was caught and disappeared.

Panic swirled into the man from Faery; he turned from that terrible spot and fled, not knowing what might be behind, but dreading it as he had never before dreaded anything, and the unknown pursued him; that terrible defence became offence and hung to his heel as a wolf pads by the flank of a bull.

And Aillen was not in his own world! He was in the world of men, where movement is not easy and the very air a burden. In his own sphere, in his own element, he might have outrun Fionn, but this was Fionn's world, Fionn's element, and the flying god was not gross enough to outstrip him. Yet what a race he gave, for it was but at the entrance to his own Shí that the pursuer got close enough. Fionn put a finger into the thong of the great spear, and at that cast night fell on Aillen mac Midna. His eyes went black, his mind whirled and ceased, there came nothingness where he had been, and as the Birgha whistled into his shoulder-blades he withered away, he tumbled emptily and was dead. Fionn took his lovely head from its shoulders and went back through the night to Tara.

Triumphant Fionn, who had dealt death to a god, and to whom death would be dealt, and who is now dead!

He reached the palace at sunrise.

On that morning all were astir early. They wished to see what destruction had been wrought by the great being, but it was young Fionn they saw and that redoubtable head swinging by its hair.

"What is your demand?" said the Ard-Rí.

"The thing that it is right I should ask," said Fionn: "the command of the Fianna of Ireland."

"Make your choice," said Conn to Goll Mor; "you will leave Ireland, or you will place your hand in the hand of this champion and be his man."

Goll could do a thing that would be hard for another person, and he could do it so beautifully that he was not diminished by any action.

"Here is my hand," said Goll.

And he twinkled at the stern, young eyes that gazed on him as he made his submission.

The Birth of Bran

Chapter 1

There are people who do not like dogs a bit—they are usually women—but in this story there is a man who did not like dogs. In fact, he hated them. When he saw one he used to go black in the face, and he threw rocks at it until it got out of sight. But the Power that protects all creatures had put a squint into this man's eye, so that he always threw crooked.

This gentleman's name was Fergus Fionnliath, and his stronghold was near the harbour of Galway. Whenever a dog barked he would leap out of his seat, and he would throw everything that he owned out of the window in the direction of the bark. He gave prizes to servants who disliked dogs, and when he heard that a man had drowned a litter of pups he used to visit that person and try to marry his daughter.

Now Fionn, the son of Uail, was the reverse of Fergus Fionnliath in this matter, for he delighted in dogs, and he knew everything about them from the setting of the first little white tooth to the rocking of the last long yellow one. He knew the affections and antipathies which are proper in a dog; the degree of obedience to which dogs may be trained without losing their honourable qualities or becoming servile and suspicious; he knew the hopes that animate them, the apprehensions which tingle in their blood, and all that is to be demanded from, or forgiven in, a paw, an ear, a nose, an eye, or a tooth; and he understood these things because he loved dogs, for it is by love alone that we understand anything.

Among the three hundred dogs which Fionn owned there were two to whom he gave an especial tenderness, and who were his daily and nightly companions. These two were Bran and Sceólan, but if a person were to guess for twenty years he would not find out why Fionn loved these two dogs and why he would never be separated from them.

Fionn's mother, Muirne, went to wide Allen of Leinster to visit her son, and she brought her young sister Tuiren with her. The mother and aunt of the great captain were well treated among the Fianna, first, because they were parents to Fionn, and second, because they were beautiful and noble women.

No words can describe how delightful Muirne was—she took the branch; and as to Tuiren, a man could not look at her without becoming angry or dejected. Her face was fresh as a spring morning; her voice more cheerful than the cuckoo calling from the branch that is highest in the hedge; and her form swayed like a reed and flowed like a river, so that each person thought she would surely flow to him.

Men who had wives of their own grew moody and downcast because they could not hope to marry her, while the bachelors of the Fianna stared at each other with truculent, bloodshot eyes, and then they gazed on Tuiren so gently that she may have imagined she was being beamed on by the mild eyes of the dawn.

It was to an Ulster gentleman, Iollan Eachtach, that she gave her love, and this chief stated his rights and qualities and asked for her in marriage.

A man who did not like dogs. In fact, he hated them. When he saw one he used to go black in the face, and he threw rocks at it until it got out of sight

Now Fionn did not dislike the men of Ulster, but either he did not know them well or else he knew them too well, for he made a curious stipulation before consenting to the marriage. He bound Iollan to return the lady if there should be occasion to think her unhappy, and Iollan agreed to do so. The sureties to this bargain were Caelte mac Ronán, Goll mac Morna, and Lugaidh. Lugaidh himself gave the bride away, but it was not a pleasant ceremony for him, because he also was in love with the lady, and he would have preferred keeping her to giving her away. When she had gone he made a poem about her, beginning:

There is no more light in the sky—

And hundreds of sad people learned the poem by heart.

Chapter 2

When Iollan and Tuiren were married they went to Ulster, and they lived together very happily. But the law of life is change; nothing continues in the same way for any length of time; happiness must become unhappiness, and will be succeeded again by the joy it had displaced. The past also must be reckoned with; it is seldom as far behind us as we could wish: it is more often in front, blocking the way, and the future trips over it just when we think that the road is clear and joy our own.

Iollan had a past. He was not ashamed of it; he merely thought it was finished, although in truth it was only beginning, for it is that perpetual beginning of the past that we call the future.

Before he joined the Fianna he had been in love with a lady of the Shí, named Uct Dealv (Fair Breast), and they had been sweethearts for years. How often he had visited his sweetheart in Faery! With what eagerness and anticipation he had gone there; the lover's whistle that he used to give was known to every person in that Shí, and he had been discussed by more than one of the delicate sweet ladies of Faery.

"That is your whistle, Fair Breast," her sister of the Shí would say.

And Uct Dealv would reply: "Yes, that is my mortal, my lover, my pulse, and my one treasure."

She laid her spinning aside, or her embroidery if she was at that, or if she were baking a cake of fine wheaten bread mixed with honey she would leave the cake to bake itself and fly to Iollan. Then they went hand in hand in the country that smells of apple-blossom and honey, looking on heavy-boughed trees and on dancing and beaming clouds. Or they stood dreaming together, locked in a clasping of arms and eyes, gazing up and down on each other, Iollan staring down into sweet grey wells that peeped and flickered under thin brows, and Uct Dealv looking up into great black ones that went dreamy and went hot in endless alternation.

Then Iollan would go back to the world of men, and Uct Dealv would return to her occupations in the Land of the Ever Young.

"What did he say?" her sister of the Shí would ask.

"He said I was the Berry of the Mountain, the Star of Knowledge, and the Blossom of the Raspberry."

"They always say the same thing," her sister pouted.

"But they look other things," Uct Dealv insisted. "They feel other things," she murmured; and an endless conversation recommenced.

Then for some time Iollan did not come to Faery, and Uct Dealv marvelled at that, while her sister made an hundred surmises, each one worse than the last.

"He is not dead or he would be here," she said. "He has forgotten you, my darling."

News was brought to Tlr na n-Og of the marriage of Iollan and Tuiren, and when Uct Dealv heard that news her heart ceased to beat for a moment, and she closed her eyes.

Then they went hand in hand in the country that smells of apple-blossom and honey

"Now!" said her sister of the Shí. "That is how long the love of a mortal lasts," she added, in the voice of sad triumph which is proper to sisters.

But on Uct Dealv there came a rage of jealousy and despair such as no person in the Shí had ever heard of, and from that moment she became capable of every ill deed; for there are two things not easily controlled, and they are hunger and jealousy. She determined that the woman who had supplanted her in Iollan's affections should rue the day she did it. She pondered and brooded revenge in her heart, sitting in thoughtful solitude and bitter collectedness until at last she had a plan.

She understood the arts of magic and shape-changing, so she changed her shape into that of Fionn's female runner, the best-known woman in Ireland; then she set out from Faery and appeared in the world. She travelled in the direction of Iollan's stronghold.

Iollan knew the appearance of Fionn's messenger, but he was surprised to see her.

She saluted him.

"Health and long life, my master."

"Health and good days," he replied. "What brings you here, dear heart?"

"I come from Fionn."

"And your message?" said he.

"The royal captain intends to visit you."

"He will be welcome," said Iollan. "We shall give him an Ulster feast."

"The world knows what that is," said the messenger courteously. "And now," she continued, "I have messages for your queen."

Tuiren then walked from the house with the messenger, but when they had gone a short distance Uct Dealv drew a hazel rod from beneath her cloak and struck it on the queen's shoulder, and on the instant Tuiren's figure trembled and quivered, and it began to whirl inwards and downwards, and she changed into the appearance of a hound.

It was sad to see the beautiful, slender dog standing shivering and astonished, and sad to see the lovely eyes that looked out pitifully in terror and amazement. But Uct Dealv did not feel sad. She clasped a chain about the hound's neck, and they set off westward towards the house of Fergus Fionnliath, who was reputed to be the unfriendliest man in the world to a dog. It was because of his reputation that Uct Dealv was bringing the hound to him. She did not want a good home for this dog: she wanted the worst home that could be found in the world, and she thought that Fergus would revenge for her the rage and jealousy which she felt towards Tuiren.

Chapter 3

As they paced along Uct Dealv railed bitterly against the hound, and shook and jerked her chain. Many a sharp cry the hound gave in that journey, many a mild lament.

"Ah, supplanter! Ah, taker of another girl's sweetheart!" said Uct Dealv fiercely. "How would your lover take it if he could see you now? How would he look if he saw your pointy ears, your long thin snout, your shivering, skinny legs, and your long grey tail. He would not love you now, bad girl!"

"Have you heard of Fergus Fionnliath," she said again, "the man who does not like dogs?"

Tuiren had indeed heard of him.

"It is to Fergus I shall bring you," cried Uct Dealv. "He will throw stones at you. You have never had a stone thrown at you. Ah, bad girl! You do not know how a stone sounds as it nips the ear with a whirling buzz, nor how jagged and heavy it feels as it thumps against a skinny leg. Robber! Mortal! Bad girl! You have never been whipped, but you will be whipped now. You shall hear the song of a lash as it curls forward and bites inward and drags backward. You shall dig up old bones stealthily at night, and chew them against famine. You shall whine and squeal at the moon, and shiver in the cold, and you will never take another girl's sweetheart again."

And it was in those terms and in that tone that she spoke to Tuiren as they journeyed forward, so that the hound trembled and shrank, and whined pitifully and in despair.

They came to Fergus Fionnliath's stronghold, and Uct Dealv demanded admittance.

"Leave that dog outside," said the servant.

"I will not do so," said the pretended messenger.

"You can come in without the dog, or you can stay out with the dog," said the surly guardian.

"By my hand," cried Uct Dealv, "I will come in with this dog, or your master shall answer for it to Fionn."

At the name of Fionn the servant almost fell out of his standing. He flew to acquaint his master, and Fergus himself came to the great door of the stronghold.

"By my faith," he cried in amazement, "it is a dog."

"A dog it is," growled the glum servant.

"Go you away," said Fergus to Uct Dealv, "and when you have killed the dog come back to me and I will give you a present."

"Life and health, my good master, from Fionn, the son of Uail, the son of Baiscne," said she to Fergus.

"Life and health back to Fionn," he replied. "Come into the house and give your message, but leave the dog outside, for I don't like dogs."

"The dog comes in," the messenger replied.

"How is that?" cried Fergus angrily.

"Fionn sends you this hound to take care of until he comes for her," said the messenger.

"I wonder at that," Fergus growled, "for Fionn knows well that there is not a man in the world has less of a liking for dogs than I have."

"However that may be, master, I have given Fionn's message, and here at my heel is the dog. Do you take her or refuse her?"

"If I could refuse anything to Fionn it would be a dog," said Fergus, "but I could not refuse anything to Fionn, so give me the hound."

Uct Dealv put the chain in his hand.

"Ah, bad dog!" said she.

And then she went away well satisfied with her revenge, and returned to her own people in the Shí.

Chapter 4

On the following day Fergus called his servant:

"Has that dog stopped shivering yet?" he asked.

"It has not, sir," said the servant.

"Bring the beast here," said his master, "for whoever else is dissatisfied Fionn must be satisfied."

The dog was brought, and he examined it with a jaundiced and bitter eye.

"It has the shivers indeed," he said.

"The shivers it has," said the servant.

"How do you cure the shivers?" his master demanded, for he thought that if the animal's legs dropped off Fionn would not be satisfied.

"There is a way," said the servant doubtfully.

"If there is a way, tell it to me," cried his master angrily.

"If you were to take the beast up in your arms and hug it and kiss it, the shivers would stop," said the man.

"Do you mean—?" his master thundered, and he stretched his hand for a club.

"I heard that," said the servant humbly.

"Take that dog up," Fergus commanded, "and hug it and kiss it, and if I find a single shiver left in the beast I'll break your head."

The man bent to the hound, but it snapped a piece out of his hand, and nearly bit his nose off as well.

"That dog doesn't like me," said the man.

"Nor do I," roared Fergus; "get out of my sight."

The man went away and Fergus was left alone with the hound, but the poor creature was so terrified that it began to tremble ten times worse than before.

"Its legs will drop off," said Fergus. "Fionn will blame me," he cried in despair.

He walked to the hound.

"If you snap at my nose, or if you put as much as the start of a tooth into the beginning of a finger!" he growled.

He picked up the dog, but it did not snap, it only trembled. He held it gingerly for a few moments.

"If it has to be hugged," he said, "I'll hug it. I'd do more than that for Fionn."

He tucked and tightened the animal into his breast, and marched moodily up and down the room. The dog's nose lay along his breast under his chin, and as he gave it dutiful hugs, one hug to every five paces, the dog put out its tongue and licked him timidly under the chin.

"Stop," roared Fergus, "stop that forever," and he grew very red in the face, and stared truculently down along his nose. A soft brown eye looked up at him and the shy tongue touched again on his chin.

"If it has to be kissed," said Fergus gloomily, "I'll kiss it; I'd do more than that for Fionn," he groaned.

He bent his head, shut his eyes, and brought the dog's jaw against his lips. And at that the dog gave little wriggles in his arms, and little barks, and little licks, so that he could scarcely hold her. He put the hound down at last.

"There is not a single shiver left in her," he said.

And that was true.

Everywhere he walked the dog followed him, giving little prances and little pats against him, and keeping her eyes fixed on his with such eagerness and intelligence that he marvelled.

"That dog likes me," he murmured in amazement.

"By my hand," he cried next day, "I like that dog."

The day after that he was calling her "My One Treasure, My Little Branch." And within a week he could not bear her to be out of his sight for an instant.

He was tormented by the idea that some evil person might throw a stone at the hound, so he assembled his servants and retainers and addressed them.

He told them that the hound was the Queen of Creatures, the Pulse of his Heart, and the Apple of his Eye, and he warned them that the person who as much as looked sideways on her, or knocked one shiver out of her, would answer for the deed with pains and indignities. He recited a list of calamities which would befall such a miscreant, and these woes began with flaying and ended with dismemberment, and had inside bits of such complicated and ingenious torment that the blood of the men who heard it ran chill in their veins, and the women of the household fainted where they stood.

Chapter 5

In course of time the news came to Fionn that his mother's sister was not living with Iollan. He at once sent a messenger calling for fulfilment of the pledge that had been given to the Fianna, and demanding the instant return of Tuiren. Iollan was in a sad condition when this demand was made. He guessed that Uct Dealv had a hand in the disappearance of his queen, and he begged that time should be given him in which to find the lost girl. He promised if he could not discover her within a certain period that he would deliver his body into Fionn's hands, and would abide by whatever judgement Fionn might pronounce. The great captain agreed to that.

"Tell the wife-loser that I will have the girl or I will have his head," said Fionn.

Iollan set out then for Faery. He knew the way, and in no great time he came to the hill where Uct Dealv was.

It was hard to get Uct Dealv to meet him, but at last she consented, and they met under the apple boughs of Faery.

"Well!" said Uct Dealv. "Ah! Breaker of Vows and Traitor to Love," said she.

"Hail and a blessing," said Iollan humbly.

"By my hand," she cried, "I will give you no blessing, for it was no blessing you left with me when we parted."

"I am in danger," said Iollan.

"What is that to me?" she replied fiercely.

"Fionn may claim my head," he murmured.

"Let him claim what he can take," said she.

"No," said Iollan proudly, "he will claim what I can give."

"Tell me your tale," said she coldly.

Iollan told his story then, and, he concluded, "I am certain that you have hidden the girl."

"If I save your head from Fionn," the woman of the Shí replied, "then your head will belong to me."

"That is true," said Iollan.

"And if your head is mine, the body that goes under it is mine. Do you agree to that?"

"I do," said Iollan.

"Give me your pledge," said Uct Dealv, "that if I save you from this danger you will keep me as your sweetheart until the end of life and time."

"I give that pledge," said Iollan.

Uct Dealv went then to the house of Fergus Fionnliath, and she broke the enchantment that was on the hound, so that Tuiren's own shape came back to her; but in the matter of two small whelps, to which the hound had given birth, the enchantment could not be broken, so they had to remain as they were. These two whelps were Bran and Sceólan. They were sent to Fionn, and he loved them for ever after, for they were loyal and affectionate, as only dogs can be, and they were as intelligent as human beings. Besides that, they were Fionn's own cousins.

Tuiren was then asked in marriage by Lugaidh who had loved her so long. He had to prove to her that he was not any other woman's sweetheart, and when he proved that they were married, and they lived happily ever after, which is the proper way to live. He wrote a poem beginning:

Lovely the day. Dear is the eye of the dawn—

And a thousand merry people learned it after him.

But as to Fergus Fionnliath, he took to his bed, and he stayed there for a year and a day suffering from blighted affection, and he would have died in the bed only that Fionn sent him a special pup, and in a week that young hound became the Star of Fortune and the very Pulse of his Heart, so that he got well again, and he also lived happily ever after.

Oisín's Mother

Chapter 1

Evening was drawing nigh, and the Fianna-Finn had decided to hunt no more that day. The hounds were whistled to heel, and a sober, homeward march began. For men will walk soberly in the evening, however they go in the day, and dogs will take the mood from their masters. They were pacing so, through the golden-shafted, tender-coloured eve, when a fawn leaped suddenly from covert, and, with that leap, all quietness vanished: the men shouted, the dogs gave tongue, and a furious chase commenced.

Fionn loved a chase at any hour, and, with Bran and Sceólan, he outstripped the men and dogs of his troop, until nothing remained in the limpid world but Fionn, the two hounds, and the nimble, beautiful fawn. These, and the occasional boulders, round which they raced, or over which they scrambled; the solitary tree which dozed aloof and beautiful in the path, the occasional clump of trees that hived sweet shadow as a hive hoards honey, and the rustling grass that stretched to infinity, and that moved and crept and swung under the breeze in endless, rhythmic billowings.

In his wildest moment Fionn was thoughtful, and now, although running hard, he was thoughtful. There was no movement of his beloved hounds that he did not know; not a twitch or fling of the head, not a cock of the ears or tail that was not significant to him. But on this chase whatever signs the dogs gave were not understood by their master.

He had never seen them in such eager flight. They were almost utterly absorbed in it, but they did not whine with eagerness, nor did they cast any glance towards him for the encouraging word which he never failed to give when they sought it.

They did look at him, but it was a look which he could not comprehend. There was a question and a statement in those deep eyes, and he could not understand what that question might be, nor what it was they sought to convey. Now and again one of the dogs turned a head in full flight, and stared, not at Fionn, but distantly backwards, over the spreading and swelling plain where their companions of the hunt had disappeared.

"They are looking for the other hounds," said Fionn.

"And yet they do not give tongue! Tongue it, a Vran!" he shouted, "Bell it out, a Heólan!"

It was then they looked at him, the look which he could not understand and had never seen on a chase. They did not tongue it, nor bell it, but they added silence to silence and speed to speed, until the lean grey bodies were one pucker and lashing of movement.

Fionn marvelled. "They do not want the other dogs to hear or to come on this chase," he murmured, and he wondered what might be passing within those slender heads.

"The fawn runs well," his thought continued. "What is it, a Vran, my heart? After her, a Heólan! Hist and away, my loves!"

"There is going and to spare in that beast yet," his mind went on. "She is not stretched to the full, nor half stretched. She may outrun even Bran," he thought ragingly.

They were racing through a smooth valley in a steady, beautiful, speedy flight when, suddenly, the fawn stopped and lay on the grass, and it lay with the calm of an animal that has no fear, and the leisure of one that is not pressed.

"Here is a change," said Fionn, staring in astonishment. "She is not winded," he said. "What is she lying down for?"

But Bran and Sceólan did not stop; they added another inch to their long-stretched easy bodies, and came up on the fawn.

"It is an easy kill," said Fionn regretfully. "They have her," he cried.

But he was again astonished, for the dogs did not kill. They leaped and played about the fawn, licking its face, and rubbing delighted noses against its neck.

Fionn came up then. His long spear was lowered in his fist at the thrust, and his sharp knife was in its sheath, but he did not use them, for the fawn and the two hounds began to play round him, and the fawn was as affectionate towards him as the hounds were; so that when a velvet nose was thrust in his palm, it was as often a fawn's muzzle as a hound's.

In that joyous company he came to wide Allen of Leinster, where the people were surprised to see the hounds and the fawn and the Chief and none other of the hunters that had set out with them.

When the others reached home, the Chief told of his chase, and it was agreed that such a fawn must not be killed, but that it should be kept and well treated, and that it should be the pet fawn of the Fianna. But some of those who remembered Bran's parentage thought that as Bran herself had come from the Shí so this fawn might have come out of the Shí also.

Chapter 2

Late that night, when he was preparing for rest, the door of Fionn's chamber opened gently and a young woman came into the room. The captain stared at her, as he well might, for he had never seen or imagined to see a woman so beautiful as this was. Indeed, she was not a woman, but a young girl, and her bearing was so gently noble, her look so modestly high, that the champion dared scarcely look at her, although he could not by any means have looked away.

As she stood within the doorway, smiling, and shy as a flower, beautifully timid as a fawn, the Chief communed with his heart.

"She is the Sky-woman of the Dawn," he said. "She is the light on the foam. She is white and odorous as an apple-blossom. She smells of spice and honey. She is my beloved beyond the women of the world. She shall never be taken from me."

And that thought was delight and anguish to him: delight because of such sweet prospect, anguish because it was not yet realised, and might not be.

As the dogs had looked at him on the chase with a look that he did not understand, so she looked at him, and in her regard there was a question that baffled him and a statement which he could not follow.

He spoke to her then, mastering his heart to do it.

"I do not seem to know you," he said.

"You do not know me indeed," she replied.

"It is the more wonderful," he continued gently, "for I should know every person that is here. What do you require from me?"

"I beg your protection, royal captain."

"I give that to all," he answered. "Against whom do you desire protection?"

The door of Fionn's chamber opened gently and a young woman came into the room

"I am in terror of the Fear Doirche."

"The Dark Man of the Shí?"

"He is my enemy," she said.

"He is mine now," said Fionn. "Tell me your story."

"My name is Saeve, and I am a woman of Faery," she commenced. "In the Shí many men gave me their love, but I gave my love to no man of my country."

"That was not reasonable," the other chided with a blithe heart.

"I was contented," she replied, "and what we do not want we do not lack. But if my love went anywhere it went to a mortal, a man of the men of Ireland."

"By my hand," said Fionn in mortal distress, "I marvel who that man can be!"

"He is known to you," she murmured. "I lived thus in the peace of Faery, hearing often of my mortal champion, for the rumour of his great deeds had gone through the Shí, until a day came when the Black Magician of the Men of God put his eye on me, and, after that day, in whatever direction I looked I saw his eye."

She stopped at that, and the terror that was in her heart was on her face.

"He is everywhere," she whispered. "He is in the bushes, and on the hill. He looked up at me from the water, and he stared down on me from the sky. His voice commands out of the spaces, and it demands secretly in the heart. He is not here or there, he is in all places at all times. I cannot escape from him," she said, "and I am afraid," and at that she wept noiselessly and stared on Fionn.

"He is my enemy," Fionn growled. "I name him as my enemy."

"You will protect me," she implored.

"Where I am let him not come," said Fionn. "I also have knowledge. I am Fionn, the son of Uail, the son of Baiscne, a man among men and a god where the gods are."

"He asked me in marriage," she continued, "but my mind was full of my own dear hero, and I refused the Dark Man."

"That was your right, and I swear by my hand that if the man you desire is alive and unmarried he shall marry you or he will answer to me for the refusal."

"He is not married," said Saeve, "and you have small control over him."

The Chief frowned thoughtfully. "Except the High King and the kings I have authority in this land."

"What man has authority over himself?" said Saeve.

"Do you mean that I am the man you seek?" said Fionn.

"It is to yourself I gave my love," she replied.

"This is good news," Fionn cried joyfully, "for the moment you came through the door I loved and desired you, and the thought that you wished for another man went into my heart like a sword."

Indeed, Fionn loved Saeve as he had not loved a woman before and would never love one again. He loved her as he had never loved anything before. He could not bear to be away from her. When he saw her he did not see the world, and when he saw the world without her it was as though he saw nothing, or as if he looked on a prospect that was bleak and depressing. The belling of a stag had been music to Fionn, but when Saeve spoke that was sound enough for him. He had loved to hear the cuckoo calling in the spring from the tree that is highest in the hedge, or the blackbird's jolly whistle in an autumn bush, or the thin, sweet enchantment that comes to the mind when a lark thrills out of sight in the air and the hushed fields listen to the song. But his wife's voice was sweeter to Fionn than the singing of a lark. She filled him with wonder and surmise. There was magic in the tips of her fingers. Her thin palm ravished him. Her slender foot set his heart beating; and whatever way her head moved there came a new shape of beauty to her face.

"She is always new," said Fionn. "She is always better than any other woman; she is always better than herself."

He attended no more to the Fianna. He ceased to hunt. He did not listen to the songs of poets or the curious sayings of magicians, for all of these were in his wife, and something that was beyond these was in her also.

"She is this world and the next one; she is completion," said Fionn.

Chapter 3

It happened that the men of Lochlann came on an expedition against Ireland. A monstrous fleet rounded the bluffs of Ben Edair, and the Danes landed there, to prepare an attack which would render them masters of the country. Fionn and the Fianna-Finn marched against them. He did not like the men of Lochlann at any time, but this time he moved against them in wrath, for not only were they attacking Ireland, but they had come between him and the deepest joy his life had known.

It was a hard fight, but a short one. The Lochlannachs were driven back to their ships, and within a week the only Danes remaining in Ireland were those that had been buried there.

That finished, he left the victorious Fianna and returned swiftly to the plain of Allen, for he could not bear to be one unnecessary day parted from Saeve.

"You are not leaving us!" exclaimed Goll mac Morna.

"I must go," Fionn replied.

"You will not desert the victory feast," Conán reproached him.

"Stay with us, Chief," Caelte begged.

"What is a feast without Fionn?" they complained.

But he would not stay.

"By my hand," he cried, "I must go. She will be looking for me from the window."

"That will happen indeed," Goll admitted.

"That will happen," cried Fionn. "And when she sees me far out on the plain, she will run through the great gate to meet me."

"It would be the queer wife would neglect that run," Conán growled.

"I shall hold her hand again," Fionn entrusted to Caelte's ear.

"You will do that, surely."

"I shall look into her face," his lord insisted. But he saw that not even beloved Caelte understood the meaning of that, and he knew sadly and yet proudly that what he meant could not be explained by any one and could not be comprehended by any one.

"You are in love, dear heart," said Caelte.

"In love he is," Conán grumbled. "A cordial for women, a disease for men, a state of wretchedness."

"Wretched in truth," the Chief murmured. "Love makes us poor. We have not eyes enough to see all that is to be seen, nor hands enough to seize the tenth of all we want. When I look in her eyes I am tormented because I am not looking at her lips, and when I see her lips my soul cries out, 'Look at her eyes, look at her eyes.' "

"That is how it happens," said Goll rememberingly.

"That way and no other," Caelte agreed.

And the champions looked backwards in time on these lips and those, and knew their Chief would go.

When Fionn came in sight of the great keep his blood and his feet quickened, and now and again he waved a spear in the air.

"She does not see me yet," he thought mournfully.

"She cannot see me yet," he amended, reproaching himself.

But his mind was troubled, for he thought also, or he felt without thinking, that had the positions been changed he would have seen her at twice the distance.

"She thinks I have been unable to get away from the battle, or that I was forced to remain for the feast."

And, without thinking it, he thought that had the positions been changed he would have known that nothing could retain the one that was absent.

"Women," he said, "are shamefaced, they do not like to appear eager when others are observing them."

But he knew that he would not have known if others were observing him, and that he would not have cared about it if he had known. And he knew that his Saeve would not have seen, and would not have cared for any eyes than his.

He gripped his spear on that reflection, and ran as he had not run in his life, so that it was a panting, dishevelled man that raced heavily through the gates of the great Dun.

Within the Dun there was disorder. Servants were shouting to one another, and women were running to and fro aimlessly, wringing their hands and screaming; and, when they saw the Champion, those nearest to him ran away, and there was a general effort on the part of every person to get behind every other person. But Fionn caught the eye of his butler, Gariv Cronán, the Rough Buzzer, and held it.

"Come you here," he said.

And the Rough Buzzer came to him without a single buzz in his body.

"Where is the Flower of Allen?" his master demanded.

"I do not know, master," the terrified servant replied.

"You do not know!" said Fionn. "Tell what you do know."

And the man told him this story.

Chapter 4

When you had been away for a day the guards were surprised. They were looking from the heights of the Dun, and the Flower of Allen was with them. She, for she had a quest's eye, called out that the master of the Fianna was coming over the ridges to the Dun, and she ran from the keep to meet you."

"It was not I," said Fionn.

"It bore your shape," replied Gariv Cronán. "It had your armour and your face, and the dogs, Bran and Sceólan, were with it."

"They were with me," said Fionn.

"They seemed to be with it," said the servant humbly.

"Tell us this tale," cried Fionn.

"We were distrustful," the servant continued. "We had never known Fionn to return from a combat before it had been fought, and we knew you could not have reached Ben Edair or encountered the Lochlannachs. So we urged our lady to let us go out to meet you, but to remain herself in the Dun."

"It was good urging," Fionn assented.

"She would not be advised," the servant wailed. "She cried to us, 'Let me go to meet my love.'"

"Alas!" said Fionn.

"She cried on us, 'Let me go to meet my husband, the father of the child that is not born.'"

"Alas!" groaned deep-wounded Fionn.

"She ran towards your appearance that had your arms stretched out to her."

At that wise Fionn put his hand before his eyes, seeing all that happened.

"Tell on your tale," said he.

"She ran to those arms, and when she reached them the figure lifted its hand. It touched her with a hazel rod, and, while we looked, she disappeared, and where she had been there was a fawn standing and shivering. The fawn turned and bounded towards the gate of the Dun, but the hounds that were by flew after her."

Fionn stared on him like a lost man.

"They took her by the throat—" the shivering servant whispered.

"Ah!" cried Fionn in a terrible voice.

"And they dragged her back to the figure that seemed to be Fionn. Three times she broke away and came bounding to us, and three times the dogs took her by the throat and dragged her back."

"You stood to look!" the Chief snarled.

"No, master, we ran, but she vanished as we got to her; the great hounds vanished away, and that being that seemed to be Fionn disappeared with them. We were left in the rough grass, staring about us and at each other, and listening to the moan of the wind and the terror of our hearts."

"Forgive us, dear master," the servant cried. But the great captain made him no answer. He stood as though he were dumb and blind, and now and again he beat terribly on his breast with his closed fist, as though he would kill that within him which should be dead and could not die. He went so, beating on his breast, to his inner room in the Dun, and he was not seen again for the rest of that day, nor until the sun rose over Moy Lifé in the morning.

Chapter 5

For many years after that time, when he was not fighting against the enemies of Ireland, Fionn was searching and hunting through the length and breadth of the country in the hope that he might again chance on his lovely lady from the Shí. Through all that time he slept in misery each night and he rose each day to grief. Whenever he hunted he brought only the hounds that he trusted, Bran and Sceólan, Lomaire, Brod, and Lomlu; for if a fawn was chased each of these five great dogs would know if that was a fawn to be killed or one to be protected, and so there was small danger to Saeve and a small hope of finding her.

Once, when seven years had passed in fruitless search, Fionn and the chief nobles of the Fianna were hunting Ben Gulbain. All the hounds of the Fianna were out, for Fionn had now given up hope of encountering the Flower of Allen. As the hunt swept along the sides of the hill there arose a great outcry of hounds from a narrow place high on the slope and, over all that uproar there came the savage baying of Fionn's own dogs.

"What is this for?" said Fionn, and with his companions he pressed to the spot whence the noise came.

"They are fighting all the hounds of the Fianna," cried a champion.

And they were. The five wise hounds were in a circle and were giving battle to an hundred dogs at once. They were bristling and terrible, and each bite from those great, keen jaws was woe to the beast that received it. Nor did they fight in silence as was their custom and training, but between each onslaught the great heads were uplifted, and they pealed loudly, mournfully, urgently, for their master.

"They are calling on me," he roared.

And with that he ran, as he had only once before run, and the men who were nigh to him went racing as they would not have run for their lives. They came to the narrow place on the slope of the mountain, and they saw the five great hounds in a circle keeping off the other dogs, and in the middle of the ring a little boy was standing. He had long, beautiful hair, and he was naked. He was not daunted by the terrible combat and clamour of the hounds. He did not look at the hounds, but he stared like a young prince at Fionn and the champions as they rushed towards him scattering the pack with the butts of their spears. When the fight was over, Bran and Sceólan ran whining to the little boy and licked his hands.

"They do that to no one," said a bystander. "What new master is this they have found?"

Fionn bent to the boy. "Tell me, my little prince and pulse, what your name is, and how you have come into the middle of a hunting-pack, and why you are naked?"

But the boy did not understand the language of the men of Ireland. He put his hand into Fionn's, and the Chief felt as if that little hand had been put into his heart. He lifted the lad to his great shoulder.

"We have caught something on this hunt," said he to Caelte mac Ronán. "We must bring this treasure home. You shall be one of the Fianna-Finn, my darling," he called upwards.

The boy looked down on him, and in the noble trust and fearlessness of that regard Fionn's heart melted away.

"My little fawn!" he said.

And he remembered that other fawn. He set the boy between his knees and stared at him earnestly and long.

"There is surely the same look," he said to his wakening heart; "that is the very eye of Saeve."

The grief flooded out of his heart as at a stroke, and joy foamed into it in one great tide. He marched back singing to the encampment, and men saw once more the merry Chief they had almost forgotten.

Chapter 6

Just as at one time he could not be parted from Saeve, so now he could not be separated from this boy. He had a thousand names for him, each one more tender than the last: "My Fawn, My Pulse, My Secret Little Treasure," or he would call him "My Music, My Blossoming Branch, My Store in the Heart, My Soul." And the dogs were as wild for the boy as Fionn was. He could sit in safety among a pack that would have torn any man to pieces, and the reason was that Bran and Sceólan, with their three whelps, followed him about like shadows. When he was with the pack these five were with him, and woeful indeed was the eye they turned on their comrades when these pushed too closely or were not properly humble. They thrashed the pack severally and collectively until every hound in Fionn's kennels knew that the little lad was their master, and that there was nothing in the world so sacred as he was.

In no long time the five wise hounds could have given over their guardianship, so complete was the recognition of their young lord. But they did not so give over, for it was not love they gave the lad but adoration.

Fionn even may have been embarrassed by their too close attendance. If he had been able to do so he might have spoken harshly to his dogs, but he could not; it was unthinkable that he should; and the boy might have spoken harshly to him if he had dared to do it. For this was the order of Fionn's affection: first there was the boy; next, Bran and Sceólan with their three whelps; then Caelte mac Ronán, and from him down through the champions. He loved them all, but it was along that precedence his affections ran. The thorn that went into Bran's foot ran into Fionn's also. The world knew it, and there was not a champion but admitted sorrowfully that there was reason for his love.

Little by little the boy came to understand their speech and to speak it himself, and at last he was able to tell his story to Fionn.

There were many blanks in the tale, for a young child does not remember very well. Deeds grow old in a day and are buried in a night. New memories come crowding on old ones, and one must learn to forget as well as to remember. A whole new life had come on this boy, a life that was instant and memorable, so that his present memories blended into and obscured the past, and he could not be quite sure if that which he told of had happened in this world or in the world he had left.

Chapter 7

"I used to live," he said, "in a wide, beautiful place. There were hills and valleys there, and woods and streams, but in whatever direction

I went I came always to a cliff, so tall it seemed to lean against the sky, and so straight that even a goat would not have imagined to climb it."

"I do not know of any such place," Fionn mused.

"There is no such place in Ireland," said Caelte, "but in the Shí there is such a place."

"There is in truth," said Fionn.

"I used to eat fruits and roots in the summer," the boy continued, "but in the winter food was left for me in a cave."

"Was there no one with you?" Fionn asked.

"No one but a deer that loved me, and that I loved."

"Ah me!" cried Fionn in anguish, "tell me your tale, my son."

"A dark stern man came often after us, and he used to speak with the deer. Sometimes he talked gently and softly and coaxingly, but at times again he would shout loudly and in a harsh, angry voice. But whatever way he talked the deer would draw away from him in dread, and he always left her at last furiously."

"It is the Dark Magician of the Men of God," cried Fionn despairingly.

"It is indeed, my soul," said Caelte.

"The last time I saw the deer," the child continued, "the dark man was speaking to her. He spoke for a long time. He spoke gently and angrily, and gently and angrily, so that I thought he would never stop talking, but in the end he struck her with a hazel rod, so that she was forced to follow him when he went away. She was looking back at me all the time and she was crying so bitterly that any one would pity her. I tried to follow her also, but I could not move, and I cried after her too, with rage and grief, until I could see her no more and hear her no more. Then I fell on the grass, my senses went away from me, and when I awoke I was on the hill in the middle of the hounds where you found me."

That was the boy whom the Fianna called Oisín, or the Little Fawn. He grew to be a great fighter afterwards, and he was the chief maker of poems in the world. But he was not yet finished with the Shí. He was to go back into Faery when the time came, and to come thence again to tell these tales, for it was by him these tales were told.

The Wooing of Becfola

Chapter 1

We do not know where Becfola came from. Nor do we know for certain where she went to. We do not even know her real name, for the name Becfola, "Dowerless" or "Small-dowered," was given to her as a nickname. This only is certain, that she disappeared from the world we know of, and that she went to a realm where even conjecture may not follow her.

It happened in the days when Dermod, son of the famous Ae of Slane, was monarch of all Ireland. He was unmarried, but he had many foster-sons, princes from the Four Provinces, who were sent by their fathers as tokens of loyalty and affection to the Ard-Rí, and his duties as a foster-father were righteously acquitted. Among the young princes of his household there was one, Crimthann, son of Ae, King of Leinster, whom the High King preferred to the others over whom he held fatherly sway. Nor was this wonderful, for the lad loved him also, and was as eager and intelligent and modest as becomes a prince.

The High King and Crimthann would often set out from Tara to hunt and hawk, sometimes unaccompanied even by a servant; and on these excursions the king imparted to his foster-son his own wide knowledge of forest craft, and advised him generally as to the bearing and duties of a prince, the conduct of a court, and the care of a people.

Dermod mac Ae delighted in these solitary adventures, and when he could steal a day from policy and affairs he would send word privily to Crimthann. The boy, having donned his hunting gear, would join the king at a place arranged between them, and then they ranged abroad as chance might direct.

On one of these adventures, as they searched a flooded river to find the ford, they saw a solitary woman in a chariot driving from the west.

"I wonder what that means?" the king exclaimed thoughtfully.

"Why should you wonder at a woman in a chariot?" his companion inquired, for Crimthann loved and would have knowledge.

"Good, my Treasure," Dermod answered, "our minds are astonished when we see a woman able to drive a cow to pasture, for it has always seemed to us that they do not drive well."

Crimthann absorbed instruction like a sponge and digested it as rapidly.

"I think that is justly said," he agreed.

"But," Dermod continued, "when we see a woman driving a chariot of two horses, then we are amazed indeed."

When the machinery of anything is explained to us we grow interested, and Crimthann became, by instruction, as astonished as the king was.

"In good truth," said he, "the woman is driving two horses."

"Had you not observed it before?" his master asked with kindly malice.

"I had observed but not noticed," the young man admitted.

"Further," said the king, "surmise is aroused in us when we discover a woman far from a house; for you will have both observed and noticed that women are home-dwellers, and that a house without a woman or a woman without a house are imperfect objects, and although they be but half observed, they are noticed on the double."

"There is no doubting it," the prince answered from a knitted and thought-tormented brow.

"We shall ask this woman for information about herself," said the king decidedly.

"Let us do so," his ward agreed.

"The king's majesty uses the words 'we' and 'us' when referring to the king's majesty," said Dermod, "but princes who do not yet rule territories must use another form of speech when referring to themselves."

"I am very thoughtless," said Crimthann humbly.

The king kissed him on both cheeks.

"Indeed, my dear heart and my son, we are not scolding you, but you must try not to look so terribly thoughtful when you think. It is part of the art of a ruler."

"I shall never master that hard art," lamented his fosterling.

"We must all master it," Dermod replied. "We may think with our minds and with our tongues, but we should never think with our noses and with our eyebrows,"

The woman in the chariot had drawn nigh to the ford by which they were standing, and, without pause, she swung her steeds into the shallows and came across the river in a tumult of foam and spray.

"Does she not drive well?" cried Crimthann admiringly.

"When you are older," the king counselled him, "you will admire that which is truly admirable, for although the driving is good the lady is better."

He continued with enthusiasm:

"She is in truth a wonder of the world and an endless delight to the eye."

She was all that and more, and, as she took the horses through the river and lifted them up the bank, her flying hair and parted lips and all the young strength and grace of her body went into the king's eye and could not easily come out again.

Nevertheless, it was upon his ward that the lady's gaze rested, and if the king could scarcely look away from her, she could, but only with an equal effort, look away from Crimthann.

"Halt there!" cried the king.

"Who should I halt for?" the lady demanded, halting all the same, as is the manner of women, who rebel against command and yet receive it.

"Halt for Dermod!"

"There are Dermods and Dermods in this world," she quoted.

"There is yet but one Ard-Rí," the monarch answered.

She then descended from the chariot and made her reverence.

"I wish to know your name?" said he.

But at this demand the lady frowned and answered decidedly:

"I do not wish to tell it."

"I wish to know also where you come from and to what place you are going?"

"I do not wish to tell any of these things."

"Not to the king?"

"I do not wish to tell them to any one."

Crimthann was scandalised.

"Lady," he pleaded, "you will surely not withhold information from the Ard-Rí?"

But the lady stared as royally on the High King as the High King did on her, and, whatever it was he saw in those lovely eyes, the king did not insist.

He drew Crimthann apart, for he withheld no instruction from that lad.

"My heart," he said, "we must always try to act wisely, and we should only insist on receiving answers to questions in which we are personally concerned."

Crimthann imbibed all the justice of that remark.

"Thus I do not really require to know this lady's name, nor do I care from what direction she comes."

"You do not?" Crimthann asked.

"No, but what I do wish to know is, Will she marry me?"

"By my hand that is a notable question," his companion stammered.

"It is a question that must be answered," the king cried triumphantly. "But," he continued, "to learn what woman she is, or where she comes from, might bring us torment as well as information. Who knows in what adventures the past has engaged her!"

And he stared for a profound moment on disturbing, sinister horizons, and Crimthann meditated there with him.

"The past is hers," he concluded, "but the future is ours, and we shall only demand that which is pertinent to the future."

He returned to the lady.

"We wish you to be our wife," he said.

And he gazed on her benevolently and firmly and carefully when he said that, so that her regard could not stray otherwhere. Yet, even as he looked, a tear did well into those lovely eyes, and behind her brow a thought moved of the beautiful boy who was looking at her from the king's side.

But when the High King of Ireland asks us to marry him we do not refuse, for it is not a thing that we shall be asked to do every day in the week, and there is no woman in the world but would love to rule it in Tara.

No second tear crept on the lady's lashes, and, with her hand in the king's hand, they paced together towards the palace, while behind them, in melancholy mood, Crimthann mac Ae led the horses and the chariot.

Chapter 2

They were married in a haste which equalled the king's desire; and as he did not again ask her name, and as she did not volunteer to give it, and as she brought no dowry to her husband and received none from him, she was called Becfola, the Dowerless.

Time passed, and the king's happiness was as great as his expectation of it had promised. But on the part of Becfola no similar tidings can be given.

There are those whose happiness lies in ambition and station, and to such a one the fact of being queen to the High King of Ireland is a satisfaction at which desire is sated. But the mind of Becfola was not of this temperate quality, and, lacking Crimthann, it seemed to her that she possessed nothing.

For to her mind he was the sunlight in the sun, the brightness in the moonbeam; he was the savour in fruit and the taste in honey; and when she looked from Crimthann to the king she could not but consider that the right man was in the wrong place. She thought that crowned only with his curls Crimthann mac Ae was more nobly diademed than are the masters of the world, and she told him so.

His terror on hearing this unexpected news was so great that he meditated immediate flight from Tara; but when a thing has been uttered once it is easier said the second time and on the third repetition it is patiently listened to.

After no great delay Crimthann mac Ae agreed and arranged that he and Becfola should fly from Tara, and it was part of their understanding that they should live happily ever after.

One morning, when not even a bird was astir, the king felt that his dear companion was rising. He looked with one eye at the light that stole greyly through the window, and recognised that it could not in justice be called light.

"There is not even a bird up," he murmured.

And then to Becfola:

"What is the early rising for, dear heart?"

"An engagement I have," she replied.

"This is not a time for engagements," said the calm monarch.

"Let it be so," she replied, and she dressed rapidly.

"And what is the engagement?" he pursued.

"Raiment that I left at a certain place and must have. Eight silken smocks embroidered with gold, eight precious brooches of beaten gold, three diadems of pure gold."

"At this hour," said the patient king, "the bed is better than the road."

"Let it be so," said she.

"And moreover," he continued, "a Sunday journey brings bad luck."

"Let the luck come that will come," she answered.

"To keep a cat from cream or a woman from her gear is not work for a king," said the monarch severely.

The Ard-Rí could look on all things with composure, and regard all beings with a tranquil eye; but it should be known that there was one deed entirely hateful to him, and he would punish its commission with the very last rigour—this was, a transgression of the Sunday. During six days of the week all that could happen might happen, so far as Dermod was concerned, but on the seventh day nothing should happen at all if the High King could restrain it. Had it been possible he would have tethered the birds to their own green branches on that day, and forbidden the clouds to pack the upper world with stir and colour. These the king permitted, with a tight lip, perhaps, but all else that came under his hand felt his control.

It was his custom when he arose on the morn of Sunday to climb to the most elevated point of Tara, and gaze thence on every side, so that he might see if any fairies or people of the Shí were disporting themselves in his lordship; for he absolutely prohibited the usage of the earth to these beings on the Sunday, and woe's worth was it for the sweet being he discovered breaking his law.

We do not know what ill he could do to the fairies, but during Dermod's reign the world said its prayers on Sunday and the Shí folk stayed in their hills.

It may be imagined, therefore, with what wrath he saw his wife's preparations for her journey, but, although a king can do everything, what can a husband do . . . ? He rearranged himself for slumber.

"I am no party to this untimely journey," he said angrily.

"Let it be so," said Becfola.

She left the palace with one maid, and as she crossed the doorway something happened to her, but by what means it happened would be hard to tell; for in the one pace she passed out of the palace and out of the world, and the second step she trod was in Faery, but she did not know this.

Her intention was to go to Cluain da chaillech to meet Crimthann, but when she left the palace she did not remember Crimthann any more.

To her eye and to the eye of her maid the world was as it always had been, and the landmarks they knew were about them. But the object for which they were travelling was different, although unknown, and the people they passed on the roads were unknown, and were yet people that they knew.

They set out southwards from Tara into the Duffry of Leinster, and after some time they came into wild country and went astray. At last Becfola halted, saying:

"I do not know where we are."

The maid replied that she also did not know.

"Yet," said Becfola, "if we continue to walk straight on we shall arrive somewhere."

They went on, and the maid watered the road with her tears.

Night drew on them; a grey chill, a grey silence, and they were enveloped in that chill and silence; and they began to go in expectation and terror, for they both knew and did not know that which they were bound for.

As they toiled desolately up the rustling and whispering side of a low hill the maid chanced to look back, and when she looked back she screamed and pointed, and clung to Becfola's arm. Becfola followed the pointing finger, and saw below a large black mass that moved jerkily forward.

"Wolves!" cried the maid.

"Run to the trees yonder," her mistress ordered. "We will climb them and sit among the branches."

They ran then, the maid moaning and lamenting all the while.

"I cannot climb a tree," she sobbed, "I shall be eaten by the wolves."

And that was true.

But her mistress climbed a tree, and drew by a hand's breadth from the rap and snap and slaver of those steel jaws. Then, sitting on a branch, she looked with angry woe at the straining and snarling

She looked with angry woe at the straining and snarling horde below

horde below, seeing many a white fang in those grinning jowls, and the smouldering, red blink of those leaping and prowling eyes.

Chapter 3

But after some time the moon arose and the wolves went away, for their leader, a sagacious and crafty chief, declared that as long as they remained where they were, the lady would remain where she was; and so, with a hearty curse on trees, the troop departed.

Becfola had pains in her legs from the way she had wrapped them about the branch, but there was no part of her that did not ache, for a lady does not sit with any ease upon a tree.

For some time she did not care to come down from the branch. "Those wolves may return," she said, "for their chief is crafty and sagacious, and it is certain, from the look I caught in his eye as he departed, that he would rather taste of me than eat any woman he has met."

She looked carefully in every direction to see if she might discover them in hiding; she looked closely and lingeringly at the shadows under distant trees to see if these shadows moved; and she listened on every wind to try if she could distinguish a yap or a yawn or a sneeze.

But she saw or heard nothing; and little by little tranquillity crept into her mind, and she began to consider that a danger which is past is a danger that may be neglected.

Yet ere she descended she looked again on the world of jet and silver that dozed about her, and she spied a red glimmer among distant trees.

"There is no danger where there is light," she said, and she thereupon came from the tree and ran in the direction that she had noted.

In a spot between three great oaks she came upon a man who was roasting a wild boar over a fire. She saluted this youth and sat beside him. But after the first glance and greeting he did not look at her again, nor did he speak.

When the boar was cooked he ate of it and she had her share. Then he arose from the fire and walked away among the trees. Becfola followed, feeling ruefully that something new to her experience had arrived; "For," she thought, "it is usual that young men should not speak to me now that I am the mate of a king, but it is very unusual that young men should not look at me."

But if the young man did not look at her she looked well at him, and what she saw pleased her so much that she had no time for further cogitation. For if Crimthann had been beautiful, this youth was ten times more beautiful. The curls on Crimthann's head had been indeed as a benediction to the queen's eye, so that she had eaten the better and slept the sounder for seeing him. But the sight of this youth left her without the desire to eat, and, as for sleep, she dreaded it, for if she closed an eye she would be robbed of the one delight in time, which was to look at this young man, and not to cease looking at him while her eye could peer or her head could remain upright.

They came to an inlet of the sea all sweet and calm under the round, silver-flooding moon, and the young man, with Becfola treading on his heel, stepped into a boat and rowed to a high-jutting, pleasant island. There they went inland towards a vast palace, in which there was no person but themselves alone, and there the young man went to sleep, while Becfola sat staring at him until the unavoidable peace pressed down her eyelids and she too slumbered.

She was awakened in the morning by a great shout.

"Come out, Flann, come out, my heart!"

The young man leaped from his couch, girded on his harness, and strode out. Three young men met him, each in battle harness, and these four advanced to meet four other men who awaited them at a

little distance on the lawn. Then these two sets of four fought together with every warlike courtesy but with every warlike severity, and at the end of that combat there was but one man standing, and the other seven lay tossed in death.

Becfola spoke to the youth.

"Your combat has indeed been gallant," she said.

"Alas," he replied, "if it has been a gallant deed it has not been a good one, for my three brothers are dead and my four nephews are dead."

"Ah me!" cried Becfola, "why did you fight that fight?"

"For the lordship of this island, the Isle of Fedach, son of Dall."

But, although Becfola was moved and horrified by this battle, it was in another direction that her interest lay; therefore she soon asked the question which lay next her heart:

"Why would you not speak to me or look at me?"

"Until I have won the kingship of this land from all claimants, I am no match for the mate of the High King of Ireland," he replied.

And that reply was like balm to the heart of Becfola.

"What shall I do?" she inquired radiantly.

"Return to your home," he counselled. "I will escort you there with your maid, for she is not really dead, and when I have won my lordship I will go seek you in Tara."

"You will surely come," she insisted.

"By my hand," quoth he, "I will come."

These three returned then, and at the end of a day and night they saw far off the mighty roofs of Tara massed in the morning haze. The young man left them, and with many a backward look and with dragging, reluctant feet, Becfola crossed the threshold of the palace, wondering what she should say to Dermod and how she could account for an absence of three days' duration.

Chapter 4

It was so early that not even a bird was yet awake, and the dull grey light that came from the atmosphere enlarged and made indistinct all that one looked at, and swathed all things in a cold and livid gloom.

As she trod cautiously through dim corridors Becfola was glad that, saving the guards, no creature was astir, and that for some time yet she need account to no person for her movements. She was glad also of a respite which would enable her to settle into her home and draw about her the composure which women feel when they are surrounded by the walls of their houses, and can see about them the possessions which, by the fact of ownership, have become almost a part of their personality. Sundered from her belongings, no woman is tranquil, her heart is not truly at ease, however her mind may function, so that under the broad sky or in the house of another she is not the competent, precise individual which she becomes when she sees again her household in order and her domestic requirements at her hand.

Becfola pushed the door of the king's sleeping chamber and entered noiselessly. Then she sat quietly in a seat gazing on the recumbent monarch, and prepared to consider how she should advance to him when he awakened, and with what information she might stay his inquiries or reproaches.

"I will reproach him," she thought. "I will call him a bad husband and astonish him, and he will forget everything but his own alarm and indignation."

But at that moment the king lifted his head from the pillow and looked kindly at her.

Her heart gave a great throb, and she prepared to speak at once and in great volume before he could formulate any question. But the king spoke first, and what he said so astonished her that the explanation and reproach with which her tongue was thrilling fled from it at a stroke, and she could only sit staring and bewildered and tongue-tied.

"Well, my dear heart," said the king, "have you decided not to keep that engagement?"

"I—I— !" Becfola stammered.

"It is truly not an hour for engagements," Dermod insisted, "for not a bird of the birds has left his tree; and," he continued maliciously, "the light is such that you could not see an engagement even if you met one."

"I," Becfola gasped. "I——!"

"A Sunday journey," he went on, "is a notoriously bad journey. No good can come from it. You can get your smocks and diadems to-morrow. But at this hour a wise person leaves engagements to the bats and the staring owls and the round-eyed creatures that prowl and sniff in the dark. Come back to the warm bed, sweet woman, and set out on your journey in the morning."

Such a load of apprehension was lifted from Becfola's heart that she instantly did as she had been commanded, and such a bewilderment had yet possession of her faculties that she could not think or utter a word on any subject.

Yet the thought did come into her head as she stretched in the warm gloom that Crimthann the son of Ae must be now attending her at Cluain da chaillech, and she thought of that young man as of something wonderful and very ridiculous, and the fact that he was waiting for her troubled her no more than if a sheep had been waiting for her or a roadside bush.

She fell asleep.

Chapter 5

In the morning as they sat at breakfast four clerics were announced, and when they entered the king looked on them with stern disapproval.

"What is the meaning of this journey on Sunday?" he demanded.

A lank-jawed, thin-browed brother, with uneasy, intertwining fingers, and a deep-set, venomous eye, was the spokesman of those four.

"Indeed," he said, and the fingers of his right hand strangled and did to death the fingers of his left hand, "indeed, we have transgressed by order."

"Explain that."

"We have been sent to you hurriedly by our master, Molasius of Devenish."

"A pious, a saintly man," the king interrupted, "and one who does not countenance transgressions of the Sunday."

"We were ordered to tell you as follows," said the grim cleric, and he buried the fingers of his right hand in his left fist, so that one could not hope to see them resurrected again.

"It was the duty of one of the Brothers of Devenish," he continued, "to turn out the cattle this morning before the dawn of day, and that Brother, while in his duty, saw eight comely young men who fought together."

"On the morning of Sunday," Dermod exploded.

The cleric nodded with savage emphasis.

"On the morning of this self-same and instant sacred day."

"Tell on," said the king wrathfully.

But terror gripped with sudden fingers at Becfola's heart.

"Do not tell horrid stories on the Sunday," she pleaded. "No good can come to any one from such a tale."

"Nay, this must be told, sweet lady," said the king.

But the cleric stared at her glumly, forbiddingly, and resumed his story at a gesture.

"Of these eight men, seven were killed."

"They are in hell," the king said gloomily.

"In hell they are," the cleric replied with enthusiasm.

"And the one that was not killed?"

"He is alive," that cleric responded.

"He would be," the monarch assented. "Tell your tale."

"Molasius had those seven miscreants buried, and he took from their unhallowed necks and from their lewd arms and from their unblessed weapons the load of two men in gold and silver treasure."

"Two men's load!" said Dermod thoughtfully.

"That much," said the lean cleric. "No more, no less. And he has sent us to find out what part of that hellish treasure belongs to the Brothers of Devenish and how much is the property of the king."

Becfola again broke in, speaking graciously, regally, hastily: "Let those Brothers have the entire of the treasure, for it is Sunday treasure, and as such it will bring no luck to any one."

The cleric again looked at her coldly, with a harsh-lidded, small-set, grey-eyed glare, and waited for the king's reply.

Dermod pondered, shaking his head as to an argument on his left side, and then nodding it again as to an argument on his right.

"It shall be done as this sweet queen advises. Let a reliquary be formed with cunning workmanship of that gold and silver, dated with my date and signed with my name, to be in memory of my grandmother who gave birth to a lamb, to a salmon, and then to my father, the Ard-Rí. And, as to the treasure that remains over, a pastoral staff may be beaten from it in honour of Molasius, the pious man."

"The story is not ended," said that glum, spike-chinned cleric.

The king moved with jovial impatience.

"If you continue it," he said, "it will surely come to an end some time. A stone on a stone makes a house, dear heart, and a word on a word tells a tale."

The cleric wrapped himself into himself, and became lean and menacing. He whispered: "Besides the young man, named Flann, who was not slain, there was another person present at the scene and the combat and the transgression of Sunday."

"Who was that person?" said the alarmed monarch.

The cleric spiked forward his chin, and then butted forward his brow.

"It was the wife of the king," he shouted. "It was the woman called Becfola. It was that woman," he roared, and he extended a lean, inflexible, unending first finger at the queen.

"Dog!" the king stammered, starting up.

"If that be in truth a woman," the cleric screamed.

"What do you mean?" the king demanded in wrath and terror.

"Either she is a woman of this world to be punished, or she is a woman of the Shí to be banished, but this holy morning she was in the Shí, and her arms were about the neck of Flann."

The king sank back in his chair stupefied, gazing from one to the other, and then turned an unseeing, fear-dimmed eye towards Becfola.

"Is this true, my pulse?" he murmured.

"It is true," Becfola replied, and she became suddenly to the king's eye a whiteness and a stare.

He pointed to the door.

"Go to your engagement," he stammered. "Go to that Flann."

"He is waiting for me," said Becfola with proud shame, "and the thought that he should wait wrings my heart."

She went out from the palace then. She went away from Tara: and in all Ireland and in the world of living men she was not seen again, and she was never heard of again.

The Little Brawl at Allen

Chapter 1

I think," said Cairell Whiteskin, "that although judgement was given against Fionn, it was Fionn had the rights of it."

"He had eleven hundred killed," said Conán amiably, "and you may call that the rights of it if you like."

"All the same—" Cairell began argumentatively.

"And it was you that commenced it," Conán continued.

"Ho! Ho!" Cairell cried. "Why, you are as much to blame as I am."

"No," said Conán, "for you hit me first."

"And if we had not been separated—" the other growled.

"Separated!" said Conán, with a grin that made his beard poke all around his face.

"Yes, separated. If they had not come between us I still think—"

"Don't think out loud, dear heart, for you and I are at peace by law."

"That is true," said Cairell, "and a man must stick by a judgement. Come with me, my dear, and let us see how the youngsters are shaping in the school. One of them has rather a way with him as a swordsman."

"No youngster is any good with a sword," Conán replied.

"You are right there," said Cairell. "It takes a good ripe man for that weapon."

"Boys are good enough with slings," Conán continued, "but except for eating their fill and running away from a fight, you can't count on boys."

The two bulky men turned towards the school of the Fianna.

It happened that Fionn mac Uail had summoned the gentlemen of the Fianna and their wives to a banquet. Everybody came, for a banquet given by Fionn was not a thing to be missed. There was Goll mor mac Morna and his people; Fionn's son Oisín and his grandson Oscar. There was Dermod of the Gay Face, Caelte mac Ronán—but indeed there were too many to be told of, for all the pillars of war and battle-torches of the Gael were there.

The banquet began.

Fionn sat in the Chief Captain's seat in the middle of the fort; and facing him, in the place of honour, he placed the mirthful Goll mac Morna; and from these, ranging on either side, the nobles of the Fianna took each the place that fitted his degree and patrimony.

After good eating, good conversation; and after good conversation, sleep—that is the order of a banquet: so when each person had been served with food to the limit of desire the butlers carried in shining and jewelled drinking-horns, each having its tide of smooth, heady liquor. Then the young heroes grew merry and audacious, the ladies became gentle and kind, and the poets became wonders of knowledge and prophecy. Every eye beamed in that assembly, and on Fionn every eye was turned continually in the hope of a glance from the great, mild hero.

Goll spoke to him across the table enthusiastically.

"There is nothing wanting to this banquet, O Chief," said he.

And Fionn smiled back into that eye which seemed a well of tenderness and friendship.

"Nothing is wanting," he replied, "but a well-shaped poem."

A crier stood up then, holding in one hand a length of coarse iron links and in the other a chain of delicate, antique silver. He shook the iron chain so that the servants and followers of the household should be silent, and he shook the silver one so that the nobles and poets should hearken also.

Fergus, called True-Lips, the poet of the Fianna-Finn, then sang of Fionn and his ancestors and their deeds. When he had finished Fionn and Oisín and Oscar and mac Lugac of the Terrible Hand gave him rare and costly presents, so that every person wondered at their munificence, and even the poet, accustomed to the liberality of kings and princes, was astonished at his gifts.

Fergus then turned to the side of Goll mac Morna, and he sang of the Forts, the Destructions, the Raids, and the Wooings of clann-Morna; and as the poems succeeded each other, Goll grew more and more jovial and contented. When the songs were finished Goll turned in his seat.

"Where is my runner?" he cried.

He had a woman runner, a marvel for swiftness and trust. She stepped forward.

"I am here, royal captain."

"Have you collected my tribute from Denmark?"

"It is here."

And, with help, she laid beside him the load of three men of doubly refined gold. Out of this treasure, and from the treasure of rings and bracelets and torques that were with him, Goll mac Morna paid Fergus for his songs, and, much as Fionn had given, Goll gave twice as much.

But, as the banquet proceeded, Goll gave, whether it was to harpers or prophets or jugglers, more than any one else gave, so that

Fionn became displeased, and as the banquet proceeded he grew stern and silent.

Chapter 2[1]

The wonderful gift-giving of Goll continued, and an uneasiness and embarrassment began to creep through the great banqueting hall.

Gentlemen looked at each other questioningly, and then spoke again on indifferent matters, but only with half of their minds. The singers, the harpers, and jugglers submitted to that constraint, so that every person felt awkward and no one knew what should be done or what would happen, and from that doubt dulness came, with silence following on its heels.

There is nothing more terrible than silence. Shame grows in that blank, or anger gathers there, and we must choose which of these is to be our master.

That choice lay before Fionn, who never knew shame.

"Goll," said he, "how long have you been taking tribute from the people of Lochlann?"

"A long time now," said Goll.

And he looked into an eye that was stern and unfriendly.

"I thought that my rent was the only one those people had to pay," Fionn continued.

"Your memory is at fault," said Goll.

"Let it be so," said Fionn. "How did your tribute arise?"

"Long ago, Fionn, in the days when your father forced war on me."

"Ah!" said Fionn.

"When he raised the High King against me and banished me from Ireland."

[1] This version of the death of Uail is not correct. Also Cnocha is not in Lochlann but in Ireland.

"Continue," said Fionn, and he held Goll's eye under the great beetle of his brow.

"I went into Britain," said Goll, "and your father followed me there. I went into White Lochlann (Norway) and took it. Your father banished me thence also."

"I know it," said Fionn.

"I went into the land of the Saxons and your father chased me out of that land. And then, in Lochlann, at the battle of Cnocha, your father and I met at last, foot to foot, eye to eye, and there, Fionn!"

"And there, Goll?"

"And there I killed your father."

Fionn sat rigid and unmoving, his face stony and terrible as the face of a monument carved on the side of a cliff.

"Tell all your tale," said he.

"At that battle I beat the Lochlannachs. I penetrated to the hold of the Danish king, and I took out of his dungeon the men who had lain there for a year and were awaiting their deaths. I liberated fifteen prisoners, and one of them was Fionn."

"It is true," said Fionn.

Goll's anger fled at the word.

"Do not be jealous of me, dear heart, for if I had twice the tribute I would give it to you and to Ireland."

But at the word jealous the Chief's anger revived.

"It is an impertinence," he cried, "to boast at this table that you killed my father."

"By my hand," Goll replied, "if Fionn were to treat me as his father did I would treat Fionn the way I treated Fionn's father."

Fionn closed his eyes and beat away the anger that was rising within him. He smiled grimly.

"If I were so minded, I would not let that last word go with you, Goll, for I have here an hundred men for every man of yours."

Goll laughed aloud.

"So had your father," he said.

Fionn's brother, Cairell Whiteskin, broke into the conversation with a harsh laugh.

"How many of Fionn's household has the wonderful Goll put down?" he cried.

But Goll's brother, bald Conán the Swearer, turned a savage eye on Cairell.

"By my weapons," said he, "there were never less than an hundred-and-one men with Goll, and the least of them could have put you down easily enough."

"Ah?" cried Cairell. "And are you one of the hundred-and-one, old scaldhead?"

"One indeed, my thick-witted, thin-livered Cairell, and I undertake to prove on your hide that what my brother said was true and that what your brother said was false."

"You undertake that," growled Cairell, and on the word he loosed a furious buffet at Conán, which Conán returned with a fist so big that every part of Cairell's face was hit with the one blow. The two then fell into grips, and went lurching and punching about the great hall. Two of Oscar's sons could not bear to see their uncle being worsted, and they leaped at Conán, and two of Goll's sons rushed at them. Then Oscar himself leaped up, and with a hammer in either hand he went battering into the melee.

"I thank the gods," said Conán, "for the chance of killing yourself, Oscar."

These two encountered then, and Oscar knocked a groan of distress out of Conán. He looked appealingly at his brother Art og mac Morna, and that powerful champion flew to his aid and wounded Oscar. Oisín, Oscar's father, could not abide that; he dashed in and quelled Art Og. Then Rough Hair mac Morna wounded Oisín and was himself tumbled by mac Lugac, who was again wounded by Gara mac Morna.

The banqueting hall was in tumult. In every part of it men were giving and taking blows. Here two champions with their arms round each other's necks were stamping round and round in a slow, sad dance. Here were two crouching against each other, looking for a soft place to hit. Yonder a big-shouldered person lifted another man in his arms and threw him at a small group that charged him. In a retired corner a gentleman stood in a thoughtful attitude while he tried to pull out a tooth that had been knocked loose.

"You can't fight," he mumbled, "with a loose shoe or a loose tooth."

"Hurry up with that tooth," the man in front of him grumbled, "for I want to knock out another one."

Pressed against the wall was a bevy of ladies, some of whom were screaming and some laughing and all of whom were calling on the men to go back to their seats.

Only two people remained seated in the hall.

Goll sat twisted round watching the progress of the brawl critically, and Fionn, sitting opposite, watched Goll.

Just then Faelan, another of Fionn's sons, stormed the hall with three hundred of the Fianna, and by this force all Goll's people were put out of doors, where the fight continued.

Goll looked then calmly on Fionn.

"Your people are using their weapons," said he.

"Are they?" Fionn inquired as calmly, and as though addressing the air.

"In the matter of weapons—!" said Goll.

And the hard-fighting pillar of battle turned to where his arms hung on the wall behind him. He took his solid, well-balanced sword in his fist, over his left arm his ample, bossy shield, and, with another side-look at Fionn, he left the hall and charged irresistibly into the fray.

The banqueting hall was in tumult

Fionn then arose. He took his accoutrements from the wall also and strode out. Then he raised the triumphant Fenian shout and went into the combat.

That was no place for a sick person to be. It was not the corner which a slender-fingered woman would choose to do up her hair; nor was it the spot an ancient man would select to think quietly in, for the tumult of sword on sword, of axe on shield, the roar of the contending parties, the crying of wounded men, and the screaming of frightened women destroyed peace, and over all was the rallying cry of Goll mac Morna and the great shout of Fionn.

Then Fergus True-Lips gathered about him all the poets of the Fianna, and they surrounded the combatants. They began to chant and intone long, heavy rhymes and incantations, until the rhythmic beating of their voices covered even the noise of war, so that the men stopped hacking and hewing, and let their weapons drop from their hands. These were picked up by the poets and a reconciliation was effected between the two parties.

But Fionn affirmed that he would make no peace with clann-Morna until the matter had been judged by the king, Cormac mac Art, and by his daughter Ailve, and by his son Cairbre of Ana Lifé and by Fintan the chief poet. Goll agreed that the affair should be submitted to that court, and a day was appointed, a fortnight from that date, to meet at Tara of the Kings for judgement. Then the hall was cleansed and the banquet recommenced.

Of Fionn's people eleven hundred of men and women were dead, while of Goll's people eleven men and fifty women were dead. But it was through fright the women died, for not one of them had a wound or a bruise or a mark.

Chapter 3

AT the end of a fortnight Fionn and Goll and the chief men of the Fianna attended at Tara. The king, his son and daughter, with Flahri, Feehal, and Fintan mac Bocna, sat in the place of judgement, and Cormac called on the witnesses for evidence.

Fionn stood up, but the moment he did so Goll mac Morna arose also.

"I object to Fionn giving evidence," said he.

"Why so?" the king asked.

"Because in any matter that concerned me Fionn would turn a lie into truth and the truth into a lie."

"I do not think that is so," said Fionn.

"You see, he has already commenced it," cried Goll.

"If you object to the testimony of the chief person present, in what way are we to obtain evidence?" the king demanded.

"I," said Goll, "will trust to the evidence of Fergus True-Lips. He is Fionn's poet, and will tell no lie against his master; he is a poet, and will tell no lie against any one."

"I agree to that," said Fionn.

"I require, nevertheless," Goll continued, "that Fergus should swear before the Court, by his gods, that he will do justice between us."

Fergus was accordingly sworn, and gave his evidence.

He stated that Fionn's brother Cairell struck Conán mac Morna, that Goll's two sons came to help Conán, that Oscar went to help Cairell, and with that Fionn's people and the clann-Morna rose at each other, and what had started as a brawl ended as a battle with eleven hundred of Fionn's people and sixty-one of Goll's people dead.

"I marvel," said the king in a discontented voice, "that, considering the numbers against them, the losses of clann-Morna should be so small."

Fionn blushed when he heard that.

Fergus replied:

"Goll mac Morna covered his people with his shield. All that slaughter was done by him."

"The press was too great," Fionn grumbled. "I could not get at him in time or—"

"Or what?" said Goll with a great laugh.

Fionn shook his head sternly and said no more.

"What is your judgement?" Cormac demanded of his fellow-judges.

Flahri pronounced first.

"I give damages to clann-Morna."

"Why?" said Cormac.

"Because they were attacked first."

Cormac looked at him stubbornly.

"I do not agree with your judgement," he said.

"What is there faulty in it?" Flahri asked.

"You have not considered," the king replied, "that a soldier owes obedience to his captain, and that, given the time and the place, Fionn was the captain and Goll was only a simple soldier."

Flahri considered the king's suggestion.

"That," he said, "would hold good for the white-striking or blows of fists, but not for the red-striking or sword-strokes."

"What is your judgement?" the king asked Feehal. Feehal then pronounced:

"I hold that clann-Morna were attacked first, and that they are to be free from payment of damages."

"And as regards Fionn?" said Cormac.

"I hold that on account of his great losses Fionn is to be exempt from payment of damages, and that his losses are to be considered as damages."

"I agree in that judgement," said Fintan.

The king and his son also agreed, and the decision was imparted to the Fianna.

"One must abide by a judgement," said Fionn.

"Do you abide by it?" Goll demanded.

"I do," said Fionn.

Goll and Fionn then kissed each other, and thus peace was made. For, notwithstanding the endless bicker of these two heroes, they loved each other well.

Yet, now that the years have gone by, I think the fault lay with Goll and not with Fionn, and that the judgement given did not consider everything. For at that table Goll should not have given greater gifts than his master and host did. And it was not right of Goll to take by force the position of greatest gift-giver of the Fianna, for there was never in the world one greater at giving gifts, or giving battle, or making poems than Fionn was.

That side of the affair was not brought before the Court. But perhaps it was suppressed out of delicacy for Fionn, for if Goll could be accused of ostentation, Fionn was open to the uglier charge of jealousy. It was, nevertheless, Goll's forward and impish temper which commenced the brawl, and the verdict of time must be to exonerate Fionn and to let the blame go where it is merited.

There is, however, this to be added and remembered, that whenever Fionn was in a tight corner it was Goll that plucked him out of it; and, later on, when time did his worst on them all and the Fianna were sent to hell as unbelievers, it was Goll mac Morna who assaulted hell, with a chain in his great fist and three iron balls swinging from it, and it was he who attacked the hosts of great devils and brought Fionn and the Fianna-Finn out with him.

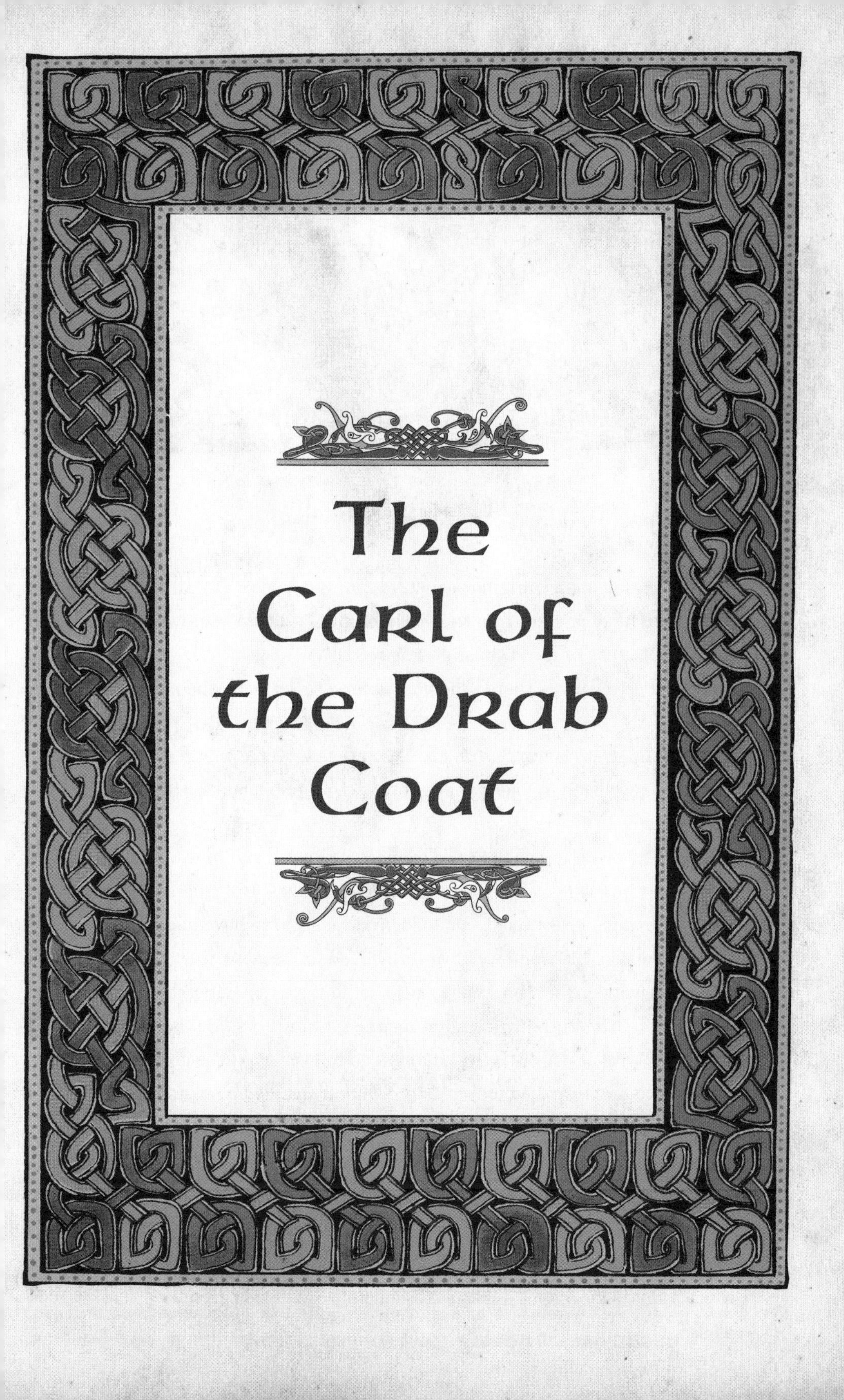

The Carl of the Drab Coat

Chapter 1

One day something happened to Fionn, the son of Uail; that is, he departed from the world of men, and was set wandering in great distress of mind through Faery. He had days and nights there and adventures there, and was able to bring back the memory of these.

That, by itself, is wonderful, for there are few people who remember that they have been to Faery or aught of all that happened to them in that state.

In truth we do not go to Faery, we become Faery, and in the beating of a pulse we may live for a year or a thousand years. But when we return the memory is quickly clouded, and we seem to have had a dream or seen a vision, although we have verily been in Faery.

It was wonderful, then, that Fionn should have remembered all that happened to him in that wide-spun moment, but in this tale there is yet more to marvel at; for not only did Fionn go to Faery, but the great army which he had marshalled to Ben Edair[1] were translated also, and neither he nor they were aware that they had departed from the world until they came back to it.

[1] The Hill of Howth

Fourteen battles, seven of the reserve and seven of the regular Fianna, had been taken by the Chief on a great march and manoeuvre. When they reached Ben Edair it was decided to pitch camp so that the troops might rest in view of the warlike plan which Fionn had imagined for the morrow. The camp was chosen, and each squadron and company of the host were lodged into an appropriate place, so there was no overcrowding and no halt or interruption of the march; for where a company halted that was its place of rest, and in that place it hindered no other company, and was at its own ease.

When this was accomplished the leaders of battalions gathered on a level, grassy plateau overlooking the sea, where a consultation began as to the next day's manoeuvres, and during this discussion they looked often on the wide water that lay wrinkling and twinkling below them.

A roomy ship under great press of sall was bearing on Ben Edair from the east.

Now and again, in a lull of the discussion, a champion would look and remark on the hurrying vessel; and it may have been during one of these moments that the adventure happened to Fionn and the Fianna.

"I wonder where that ship comes from?" said Conán idly.

But no person could surmise anything about it beyond that it was a vessel well equipped for war.

As the ship drew by the shore the watchers observed a tall man swing from the side by means of his spear shafts, and in a little while this gentleman was announced to Fionn, and was brought into his presence.

A sturdy, bellicose, forthright personage he was indeed. He was equipped in a wonderful solidity of armour, with a hard, carven helmet on his head, a splendid red-bossed shield swinging on his shoulder, a wide-grooved, straight sword clashing along his thigh. On his shoulders under the shield he carried a splendid scarlet mantle; over his breast was a great brooch of burnt gold, and in his fist he gripped a pair of thick-shafted, unburnished spears.

Fionn and the champions looked on this gentleman, and they admired exceedingly his bearing and equipment.

"Of what blood are you, young gentleman?" Fionn demanded, "and from which of the four corners of the world do you come?"

"My name is Cael of the Iron," the stranger answered, "and I am son to the King of Thessaly."

"What errand has brought you here?"

"I do not go on errands," the man replied sternly, "but on the affairs that please me."

"Be it so. What is the pleasing affair which brings you to this land?"

"Since I left my own country I have not gone from a land or an island until it paid tribute to me and acknowledged my lordship."

"And you have come to this realm—" cried Fionn, doubting his ears.

"For tribute and sovereignty," growled that other, and he struck the haft of his spear violently on the ground.

"By my hand," said Conán, "we have never heard of a warrior, however great, but his peer was found in Ireland, and the funeral songs of all such have been chanted by the women of this land."

"By my hand and word," said the harsh stranger, "your talk makes me think of a small boy or of an idiot."

"Take heed, sir," said Fionn, "for the champions and great dragons of the Gael are standing by you, and around us there are fourteen battles of the Fianna of Ireland."

"If all the Fianna who have died in the last seven years were added to all that are now here," the stranger asserted, "I would treat all of these and those grievously, and would curtail their limbs and their lives."

"It is no small boast," Conán murmured, staring at him.

"It is no boast at all," said Cael, "and, to show my quality and standing, I will propose a deed to you."

"Give out your deed," Fionn commanded.

"Thus," said Cael with cold savagery. "If you can find a man among your fourteen battalions who can outrun or outwrestle or outfight me, I will take myself off to my own country, and will trouble you no more."

And so harshly did he speak, and with such a belligerent eye did he stare, that dismay began to seize on the champions, and even Fionn felt that his breath had halted.

"It is spoken like a hero," he admitted after a moment, "and if you cannot be matched on those terms it will not be from a dearth of applicants."

"In running alone," Fionn continued thoughtfully, "we have a notable champion, Caelte mac Ronán."

"This son of Ronán will not long be notable," the stranger asserted.

"He can outstrip the red deer," said Conán.

"He can outrun the wind," cried Fionn.

"He will not be asked to outrun the red deer or the wind," the stranger sneered. "He will be asked to outrun me," he thundered. "Produce this runner, and we shall discover if he keeps as great heart in his feet as he has made you think."

"He is not with us," Conán lamented.

"These notable warriors are never with us when the call is made," said the grim stranger.

"By my hand," cried Fionn, "he shall be here in no great time, for I will fetch him myself."

"Be it so," said Cael.

"And during my absence," Fionn continued, "I leave this as a compact, that you make friends with the Fianna here present, and that you observe all the conditions and ceremonies of friendship."

Cael agreed to that.

"I will not hurt any of these people until you return," he said.

Fionn then set out towards Tara of the Kings, for he thought Caelte mac Ronán would surely be there; "and if he is not there," said

the champion to himself, "then I shall find him at Cesh Corran of the Fianna."

Chapter 2

He had not gone a great distance from Ben Edair when he came to an intricate, gloomy wood, where the trees grew so thickly and the undergrowth was such a sprout and tangle that one could scarcely pass through it. He remembered that a path had once been hacked through the wood, and he sought for this. It was a deeply scooped, hollow way, and it ran or wriggled through the entire length of the wood.

Into this gloomy drain Fionn descended and made progress, but when he had penetrated deeply in the dank forest he heard a sound of thumping and squelching footsteps, and he saw coming towards him a horrible, evil-visaged being; a wild, monstrous, yellow-skinned, big-boned giant, dressed in nothing but an ill-made, mud-plastered, drab-coloured coat, which swaggled and clapped against the calves of his big bare legs. On his stamping feet there were great brogues of boots that were shaped like, but were bigger than, a boat, and each time he put a foot down it squashed and squirted a barrelful of mud from the sunk road.

Fionn had never seen the like of this vast person, and he stood gazing on him, lost in a stare of astonishment.

The great man saluted him.

"All alone, Fionn?" he cried. "How does it happen that not one Fenian of the Fianna is at the side of his captain?"

At this inquiry Fionn got back his wits.

"That is too long a story and it is too intricate and pressing to be told, also I have no time to spare now."

"Yet tell it now," the monstrous man insisted.

Fionn, thus pressed, told of the coming of Cael of the Iron, of the challenge the latter had issued, and that he, Fionn, was off to Tara of the Kings to find Caelte mac Ronán.

"I know that foreigner well," the big man commented.

"Is he the champion he makes himself out to be?" Fionn inquired.

"He can do twice as much as he said he would do," the monster replied.

"He won't outrun Caelte mac Ronán," Fionn asserted.

The big man jeered.

"Say that he won't outrun a hedgehog, dear heart. This Cael will end the course by the time your Caelte begins to think of starting."

"Then," said Fionn, "I no longer know where to turn, or how to protect the honour of Ireland."

"I know how to do these things," the other man commented with a slow nod of the head.

"If you do," Fionn pleaded, "tell it to me upon your honour."

"I will do that," the man replied.

"Do not look any further for the rusty-kneed, slow-trotting son of Ronán," he continued, "but ask me to run your race, and, by this hand, I will be first at the post."

At this the Chief began to laugh.

"My good friend, you have work enough to carry the two tons of mud that are plastered on each of your coat-tails, to say nothing of your weighty boots."

"By my hand," the man cried, "there is no person in Ireland but myself can win that race. I claim a chance."

Fionn agreed then. "Be it so," said he. "And now, tell me your name?"

"I am known as the Carl of the Drab Coat."

"All names are names," Fionn responded, "and that also is a name."

They returned then to Ben Edair.

Chapter 3

When they came among the host the men of Ireland gathered about the vast stranger; and there were some who hid their faces in their mantles so that they should not be seen to laugh, and there were some who rolled along the ground in merriment, and there were others who could only hold their mouths open and crook their knees and hang their arms and stare dumbfoundedly upon the stranger, as though they were utterly dazed.

Cael of the Iron came also on the scene, and he examined the stranger with close and particular attention.

"What in the name of the devil is this thing?" he asked of Fionn.

"Dear heart," said Fionn, "this is the champion I am putting against you in the race."

Cael of the Iron grew purple in the face, and he almost swallowed his tongue through wrath.

"Until the end of eternity," he roared, "and until the very last moment of doom I will not move one foot in a race with this greasy, big-hoofed, ill-assembled resemblance of a beggarman."

But at this the Carl burst into a roar of laughter, so that the eardrums of the warriors present almost burst inside of their heads.

"Be reassured, my darling, I am no beggarman, and my quality is not more gross than is the blood of the most delicate prince in this assembly. You will not evade your challenge in that way, my love, and you shall run with me or you shall run to your ship with me behind you. What length of course do you propose, dear heart?"

"I never run less than sixty miles," Cael replied sullenly.

"It is a small run," said the Carl, "but it will do. From this place to the Hill of the Rushes, Slieve Luachra of Munster, is exactly sixty miles. Will that suit you?"

"I don't care how it is done," Cael answered.

"Then," said the Carl, "we may go off to Slieve Luachra now, and in the morning we can start our race there to here."

"Let it be done that way," said Cael.

These two set out then for Munster, and as the sun was setting they reached Slieve Luachra and prepared to spend the night there.

Chapter 4

Cael, my pulse," said the Carl, "we had better build a house or a hut to pass the night in."

"I'll build nothing," Cael replied, looking on the Carl with great disfavour.

"No!"

"I won't build house or hut for the sake of passing one night here, for I hope never to see this place again."

"I'll build a house myself," said the Carl, "and the man who does not help in the building can stay outside of the house."

The Carl stumped to a near-by wood, and he never rested until he had felled and tied together twenty-four couples of big timber. He thrust these under one arm and under the other he tucked a bundle of rushes for his bed, and with that one load he rushed up a house, well thatched and snug, and with the timber that remained over he made a bonfire on the floor of the house.

His companion sat at a distance regarding the work with rage and aversion.

"Now, Cael, my darling," said the Carl, "if you are a man help me to look for something to eat, for there is game here."

"Help yourself," roared Cael, "for all that I want is not to be near you."

"The tooth that does not help gets no helping," the other replied.

In a short time the Carl returned with a wild boar which he had run down. He cooked the beast over his bonfire and ate one half of it, leaving the other half for his breakfast. Then he lay down on the rushes, and in two turns he fell asleep.

But Cael lay out on the side of the hill, and if he went to sleep that night he slept fasting. It was he, however, who awakened the Carl in the morning.

"Get up, beggarman, if you are going to run against me."

The Carl rubbed his eyes.

"I never get up until I have had my fill of sleep, and there is another hour of it due to me. But if you are in a hurry, my delight, you can start running now with a blessing. I will trot on your track when I waken up."

Cael began to race then, and he was glad of the start, for his antagonist made so little account of him that he did not know what to expect when the Carl would begin to run.

"Yet," said Cael to himself, "with an hour's start the beggarman will have to move his bones if he wants to catch on me," and he settled down to a good, pelting race.

Chapter 5

At the end of an hour the Carl awoke. He ate the second half of the boar, and he tied the unpicked bones in the tail of his coat. Then with a great rattling of the boar's bones he started.

It is hard to tell how he ran or at what speed he ran, but he went forward in great two-legged jumps, and at times he moved in immense one-legged, mud-spattering hops, and at times again, with wide-stretched, far-flung, terrible-tramping, space-destroying legs he ran.

He left the swallows behind as if they were asleep. He caught up on a red deer, jumped over it, and left it standing. The wind was always behind him, for he outran it every time; and he caught up in jumps and bounces on Cael of the Iron, although Cael was running

well, with his fists up and his head back and his two legs flying in and out so vigorously that you could not see them because of that speedy movement.

Trotting by the side of Cael, the Carl thrust a hand into the tail of his coat and pulled out a fistfull of red bones.

"Here, my heart, is a meaty bone," said he, "for you fasted all night, poor friend, and if you pick a bit off the bone your stomach will get a rest."

"Keep your filth, beggarman," the other replied, "for I would rather be hanged than gnaw on a bone that you have browsed."

"Why don't you run, my pulse?" said the Carl earnestly; "why don't you try to win the race?"

Cael then began to move his limbs as if they were the wings of a fly, or the fins of a little fish, or as if they were the six legs of a terrified spider.

"I am running," he gasped.

"But try and run like this," the Carl admonished, and he gave a wriggling bound and a sudden outstretching and scurrying of shanks, and he disappeared from Cael's sight in one wild spatter of big boots.

Despair fell on Cael of the Iron, but he had a great heart.

"I will run until I burst," he shrieked, "and when I burst, may I burst to a great distance, and may I trip that beggarman up with my burstings and make him break his leg."

He settled then to a determined, savage, implacable trot.

He caught up on the Carl at last, for the latter had stopped to eat blackberries from the bushes on the road, and when he drew nigh, Cael began to jeer and sneer angrily at the Carl.

"Who lost the tails of his coat?" he roared.

"Don't ask riddles of a man that's eating blackberries," the Carl rebuked him.

“The dog without a tail and the coat without a tail,” cried Cael.

“I give it up,” the Carl mumbled.

“It’s yourself, beggarman,” jeered Cael.

“I am myself,” the Carl gurgled through a mouthful of blackberries, “and as I am myself, how can it be myself? That is a silly riddle,” he burbled.

“Look at your coat, tub of grease!”

The Carl did so.

“My faith,” said he, “where are the two tails of my coat?”

“I could smell one of them and it wrapped around a little tree thirty miles back,” said Cael, “and the other one was dishonouring a bush ten miles behind that.”

“It is bad luck to be separated from the tails of your own coat,” the Carl grumbled. “I’ll have to go back for them. Wait here, beloved, and eat blackberries until I come back, and we’ll both start fair.”

“Not half a second will I wait,” Cael replied, and he began to run towards Ben Edair as a lover runs to his maiden or as a bee flies to his hive.

“I haven’t had half my share of blackberries either,” the Carl lamented as he started to run backwards for his coat-tails.

He ran determinedly on that backward journey, and as the path he had travelled was beaten out as if it had been trampled by an hundred bulls yoked neck to neck, he was able to find the two bushes and the two coat-tails. He sewed them on his coat.

Then he sprang up, and he took to a fit and a vortex and an exasperation of running for which no description may be found. The thumping of his big boots grew as continuous as the pattering of hailstones on a roof, and the wind of his passage blew trees down. The beasts that were ranging beside his path dropped dead from concussion, and the steam that snored from his nose blew birds into bits and made great lumps of cloud fall out of the sky.

The thumping of his big boots grew as continuous as the pattering of hailstones on a roof, and the wind of his passage blew trees down

He again caught up on Cael, who was running with his head down and his toes up.

"If you won't try to run, my treasure," said the Carl, "you will never get your tribute."

And with that he incensed and exploded himself into an eye-blinding, continuous waggle and complexity of boots that left Cael behind him in a flash.

"I will run until I burst," sobbed Cael, and he screwed agitation and despair into his legs until he hummed and buzzed like a blue-bottle on a window.

Five miles from Ben Edair the Carl stopped, for he had again come among blackberries.

He ate of these until he was no more than a sack of juice, and when he heard the humming and buzzing of Cael of the Iron he mourned and lamented that he could not wait to eat his fill. He took off his coat, stuffed it full of blackberries, swung it on his shoulders, and went bounding stoutly and nimbly for Ben Edair.

Chapter 6

It would be hard to tell of the terror that was in Fionn's breast and in the hearts of the Fianna while they attended the conclusion of that race.

They discussed it unendingly, and at some moment of the day a man upbraided Fionn because he had not found Caelte the son of Ronán as had been agreed on.

"There is no one can run like Caelte," one man averred.

"He covers the ground," said another.

"He is light as a feather."

"Swift as a stag."

"Lunged like a bull."

"Legged like a wolf."

"He runs!"

These things were said to Fionn, and Fionn said these things to himself.

With every passing minute a drop of lead thumped down into every heart, and a pang of despair stabbed up to every brain.

"Go," said Fionn to a hawk-eyed man, "go to the top of this hill and watch for the coming of the racers."

And he sent lithe men with him so that they might run back in endless succession with the news.

The messengers began to run through his tent at minute intervals calling "nothing," "nothing," "nothing," as they paused and darted away.

And the words, "nothing, nothing, nothing," began to drowse into the brains of every person present.

"What can we hope from that Carl?" a champion demanded savagely.

"Nothing," cried a messenger who stood and sped.

"A clump!" cried a champion.

"A hog!" said another.

"A flat-footed,"

"Little-winded,"

"Big-bellied,"

"Lazy-boned,"

"Pork!"

"Did you think, Fionn, that a whale could swim on land, or what did you imagine that lump could do?"

"Nothing," cried a messenger, and was sped as he spoke.

Rage began to gnaw in Fionn's soul, and a red haze danced and flickered before his eyes. His hands began to twitch and a desire crept over him to seize on champions by the neck, and to shake and worry and rage among them like a wild dog raging among sheep.

He looked on one, and yet he seemed to look on all at once.

"Be silent," he growled. "Let each man be silent as a dead man."

And he sat forward, seeing all, seeing none, with his mouth drooping open, and such a wildness and bristle lowering from that great glum brow that the champions shivered as though already in the chill of death, and were silent.

He rose and stalked to the tent-door.

"Where to, O Fionn?" said a champion humbly.

"To the hill-top," said Fionn, and he stalked on.

They followed him, whispering among themselves, keeping their eyes on the ground as they climbed.

Chapter 7

What do you see?" Fionn demanded of the watcher.

"Nothing," that man replied.

"Look again," said Fionn.

The eagle-eyed man lifted a face, thin and sharp as though it had been carven on the wind, and he stared forward with an immobile intentness.

"What do you see?" said Fionn.

"Nothing," the man replied.

"I will look myself," said Fionn, and his great brow bent forward and gloomed afar.

The watcher stood beside, staring with his tense face and unwinking, lidless eye.

"What can you see, O Fionn?" said the watcher.

"I can see nothing," said Fionn, and he projected again his grim, gaunt forehead. For it seemed as if the watcher stared with his whole face, aye, and with his hands; but Fionn brooded weightedly on distance with his puckered and crannied brow.

They looked again.

"What can you see?" said Fionn.

"I see nothing," said the watcher.

"I do not know if I see or if I surmise, but something moves," said Fionn. "There is a trample," he said.

The watcher became then an eye, a rigidity, an intense out-thrusting and ransacking of thin-spun distance. At last he spoke.

"There is a dust," he said.

And at that the champions gazed also, straining hungrily afar, until their eyes became filled with a blue darkness and they could no longer see even the things that were close to them.

"I," cried Conán triumphantly, "I see a dust."

"And I," cried another.

"And I."

"I see a man," said the eagle-eyed watcher.

And again they stared, until their straining eyes grew dim with tears and winks, and they saw trees that stood up and sat down, and fields that wobbled and spun round and round in a giddily swirling world.

"There *is* a man," Conán roared.

"A man there is," cried another.

"And he is carrying a man on his back," said the watcher.

"It is Cael of the Iron carrying the Carl on his back," he groaned.

"The great pork!" a man gritted.

"The no-good!" sobbed another.

"The lean-hearted,"

"Thick-thighed,"

"Ramshackle,"

"Muddle-headed,"

"Hog!" screamed a champion.

And he beat his fists angrily against a tree.

But the eagle-eyed watcher watched until his eyes narrowed and became pin-points, and he ceased to be a man and became an optic.

"Wait," he breathed, "wait until I screw into one other inch of sight."

And they waited, looking no longer on that scarcely perceptible speck in the distance, but straining upon the eye of the watcher as though they would penetrate it and look through it.

"It is the Carl," he said, "carrying something on his back, and behind him again there is a dust."

"Are you sure?" said Fionn in a voice that rumbled and vibrated like thunder.

"It is the Carl," said the watcher, "and the dust behind him is Cael of the Iron trying to catch him up."

Then the Fianna gave a roar of exultation, and each man seized his neighbour and kissed him on both cheeks; and they gripped hands about Fionn, and they danced round and round in a great circle, roaring with laughter and relief, in the ecstasy which only comes where grisly fear has been and whence that bony jowl has taken itself away.

Chapter 8

The Carl of the Drab Coat came bumping and stumping and clumping into the camp, and was surrounded by a multitude that adored him and hailed him with tears.

"Meal!" he bawled, "meal for the love of the stars!"

And he bawled, "Meal, meal!" until he bawled everybody into silence.

Fionn addressed him.

"What for the meal, dear heart?"

"For the inside of my mouth," said the Carl, "for the recesses and crannies and deep-down profundities of my stomach. Meal, meal!" he lamented.

Meal was brought.

The Carl put his coat on the ground, opened it carefully, and revealed a store of blackberries, squashed, crushed, mangled, democratic, ill-looking.

"The meal!" he groaned, "the meal!"

It was given to him.

"What of the race, my pulse?" said Fionn.

"Wait, wait," cried the Carl. "I die, I die for meal and blackberries."

Into the centre of the mess of blackberries he discharged a barrel of meal, and be mixed the two up and through, and round and down, until the pile of white-black, red-brown slibber-slobber reached up to his shoulders. Then he commenced to paw and impel and project and cram the mixture into his mouth, and between each mouthful he sighed a contented sigh, and during every mouthful he gurgled an oozy gurgle.

But while Fionn and the Fianna stared like lost minds upon the Carl, there came a sound of buzzing, as if a hornet or a queen of the wasps or a savage, steep-winged griffin was hovering about them, and looking away they saw Cael of the Iron charging on them with a monstrous extension and scurry of his legs. He had a sword in his hand, and there was nothing in his face but redness and ferocity.

Fear fell like night around the Fianna, and they stood with slack knees and hanging hands waiting for death. But the Carl lifted a pawful of his oozy slop and discharged this at Cael with such a smash that the man's head spun off his shoulders and hopped along the ground. The Carl then picked up the head and threw it at the body with such aim and force that the neck part of the head jammed into the neck part of the body and stuck there, as good a head as ever, you would have said, but that it had got twisted the wrong way round. The Carl then lashed his opponent hand and foot.

"Now, dear heart, do you still claim tribute and lordship of Ireland?" said he.

"Let me go home," groaned Cael, "I want to go home."

"Swear by the sun and moon, if I let you go home, that you will send to Fionn, yearly and every year, the rent of the land of Thessaly."

"I swear that," said Cael, "and I would swear anything to get home."

The Carl lifted him then and put him sitting into his ship. Then he raised his big boot and gave the boat a kick that drove it seven leagues out into the sea, and that was how the adventure of Cael of the Iron finished.

"Who are you, sir?" said Fionn to the Carl.

But before answering the Carl's shape changed into one of splendour and delight.

"I am ruler of the Shí of Rath Cruachan," he said.

Then Fionn mac Uail made a feast and a banquet for the jovial god, and with that the tale is ended of the King of Thessaly's son and the Carl of the Drab Coat.

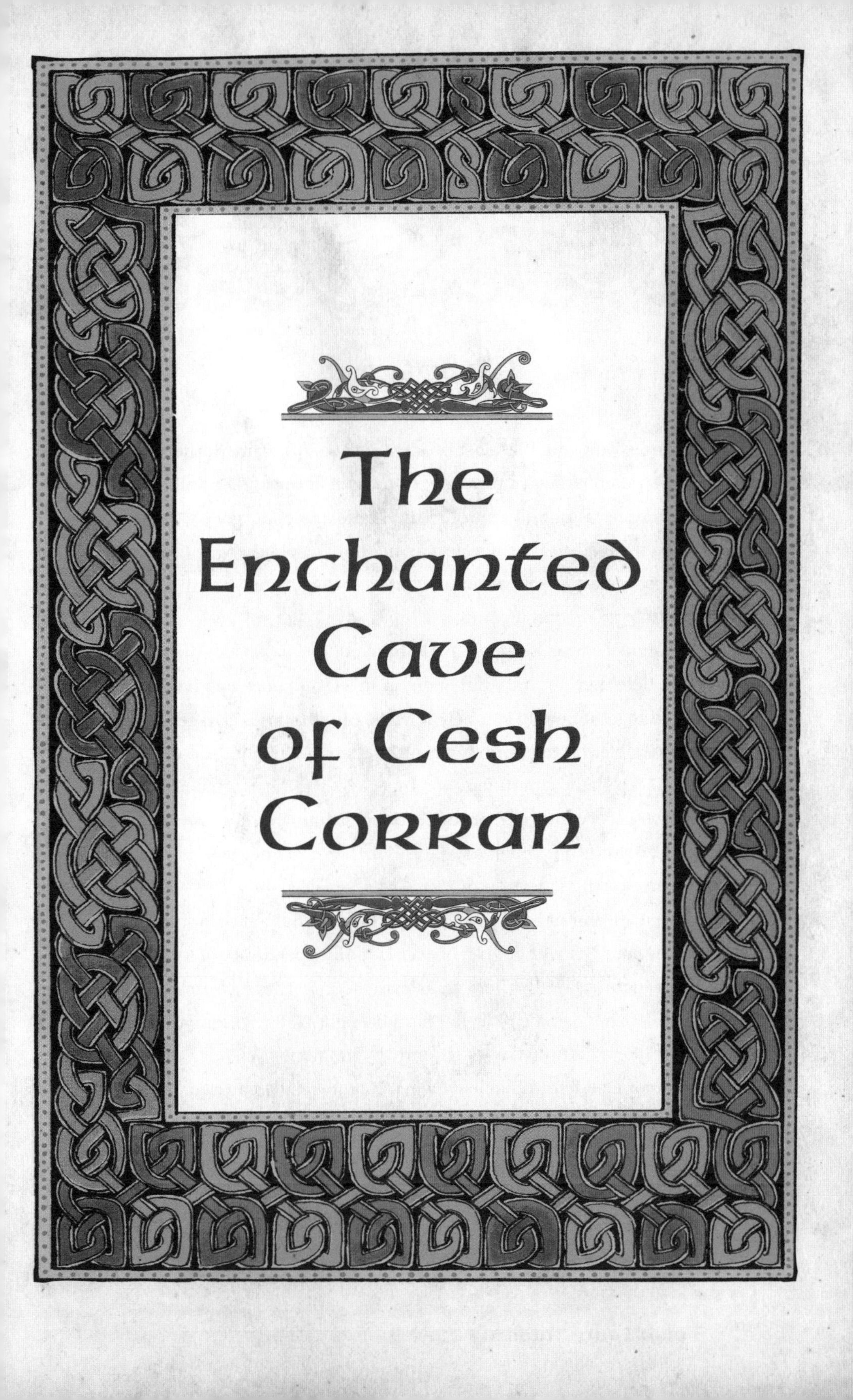
The Enchanted Cave of Cesh Corran

Chapter 1

Fionn mac Uail was the most prudent chief of an army in the world, but he was not always prudent on his own account. Discipline sometimes irked him, and he would then take any opportunity that presented for an adventure; for he was not only a soldier, he was a poet also, that is, a man of science, and whatever was strange or unusual had an irresistible attraction for him.

Such a soldier was he that, single-handed, he could take the Fianna out of any hole they got into, but such an inveterate poet was he that all the Fianna together could scarcely retrieve him from the abysses into which he tumbled. It took him to keep the Fianna safe, but it took all the Fianna to keep their captain out of danger. They did not complain of this, for they loved every hair of Fionn's head more than they loved their wives and children, and that was reasonable, for there was never in the world a person more worthy of love than Fionn was.

Goll mac Morna did not admit so much in words, but he admitted it in all his actions, for although he never lost an opportunity of killing a member of Fionn's family (there was deadly feud between clann-Baiscne and clann-Morna), yet a call from Fionn brought Goll raging to his assistance like a lion that rages tenderly by his mate. Not even a call was necessary, for Goll felt in his heart when Fionn was threatened, and he would leave Fionn's own brother only half-killed to fly where his arm was wanted. He was never thanked, of course, for although Fionn loved Goll he did not like him, and that was how Goll felt towards Fionn.

Fionn, with Conán the Swearer and the dogs Bran and Sceólan, was sitting on the hunting-mound at the top of Cesh Corran. Below and around on every side the Fianna were beating the coverts in Legney and Brefny, ranging the fastnesses of Glen Dallan, creeping in the nut and beech forests of Carbury, spying among the woods of Kyle Conor, and ranging the wide plain of Moy Conal.

The great captain was happy: his eyes were resting on the sights he liked best—the sunlight of a clear day, the waving trees, the pure sky, and the lovely movement of the earth; and his ears were filled with delectable sounds—the baying of eager dogs, the clear calling of young men, the shrill whistling that came from every side, and each sound of which told a definite thing about the hunt. There was also the plunge and scurry of the deer, the yapping of badgers, and the whirr of birds driven into reluctant flight.

Chapter 2

Now the king of the Shí of Cesh Corran, Conaran, son of Imidel, was also watching the hunt, but Fionn did not see him, for we cannot see the people of Faery until we enter their realm, and Fionn was not thinking of Faery at that moment. Conaran did not like Fionn, and, seeing that the great champion was alone, save for Conán and the two hounds Bran and Sceólan, he thought the time had come to get Fionn into his power. We do not know what Fionn had done to Conaran, but it must have been bad enough, for the king of the Shí of Cesh Corran was filled with joy at the sight of Fionn thus close to him, thus unprotected, thus unsuspicious.

This Conaran had four daughters. He was fond of them and proud of them, but if one were to search the Shís of Ireland or the land of Ireland, the equal of these four would not be found for ugliness and bad humour and twisted temperaments.

Their hair was black as ink and tough as wire: it stuck up and poked out and hung down about their heads in bushes and spikes and tangles. Their eyes were bleary and red. Their mouths were black and twisted, and in each of these mouths there was a hedge of curved yellow fangs. They had long scraggy necks that could turn all the way round like the neck of a hen. Their arms were long and skinny and muscular, and at the end of each finger they had a spiked nail that was as hard as horn and as sharp as a briar. Their bodies were covered with a bristle of hair and fur and fluff, so that they looked like dogs in some parts and like cats in others, and in other parts again they looked like chickens. They had moustaches poking under their noses and woolly wads growing out of their ears, so that when you looked at them the first time you never wanted to look at them again, and if you had to look at them a second time you were likely to die of the sight.

They were called Caevóg, Cuillen, and Iaran. The fourth daughter, Iarnach, was not present at that moment, so nothing need be said of her yet.

Conaran called these three to him.

"Fionn is alone," said he. "Fionn is alone, my treasures."

"Ah!" said Caevóg, and her jaw crunched upwards and stuck outwards, as was usual with her when she was satisfied.

"When the chance comes take it," Conaran continued, and he smiled a black, beetle-browed, unbenevolent smile.

"It's a good word," quoth Cuillen, and she swung her jaw loose and made it waggle up and down, for that was the way she smiled.

"And here is the chance," her father added.

"The chance is here," Iaran echoed, with a smile that was very like her sister's, only that it was worse, and the wen that grew on her nose joggled to and fro and did not get its balance again for a long time.

Then they smiled a smile that was agreeable to their own eyes, but which would have been a deadly thing for anybody else to see.

"But Fionn cannot see us," Caevóg objected, and her brow set downwards and her chin set upwards and her mouth squeezed sidewards, so that her face looked like a badly disappointed nut.

"And we are worth seeing," Cuillen continued, and the disappointment that was set in her sister's face got carved and twisted into hers, but it was worse in her case.

"That is the truth," said Iaran in a voice of lamentation, and her face took on a gnarl and a writhe and a solidity of ugly woe that beat the other two and made even her father marvel.

"He cannot see us now," Conaran replied, "but he will see us in a minute."

"Won't Fionn be glad when he sees us!" said the three sisters.

And then they joined hands and danced joyfully around their father, and they sang a song, the first line of which is:

Fionn thinks he is safe. But who knows when the sky will fall?

Lots of the people in the Shí learned that song by heart, and they applied it to every kind of circumstance.

Chapter 3

By his arts Conaran changed the sight of Fionn's eyes, and he did the same for Conán.

In a few minutes Fionn stood up from his place on the mound. Everything was about him as before, and he did not know that he had gone into Faery. He walked for a minute up and down the hillock. Then, as by chance, he stepped down the sloping end of the mound and stood with his mouth open, staring. He cried out:

"Come down here, Conán, my darling."

Conán stepped down to him.

"Am I dreaming?" Fionn demanded, and he stretched out his finger before him.

"If you are dreaming," said Conán, "I'm dreaming too. They weren't here a minute ago," he stammered.

Fionn looked up at the sky and found that it was still there. He stared to one side and saw the trees of Kyle Conor waving in the distance. He bent his ear to the wind and heard the shouting of hunters, the yapping of dogs, and the clear whistles, which told how the hunt was going.

"Well!" said Fionn to himself.

"By my hand!" quoth Conán to his own soul.

And the two men stared into the hillside as though what they were looking at was too wonderful to be looked away from.

"Who are they?" said Fionn.

"What are they?" Conán gasped. And they stared again.

For there was a great hole like a doorway in the side of the mound, and in that doorway the daughters of Conaran sat spinning. They had three crooked sticks of holly set up before the cave, and they were reeling yarn off these. But it was enchantment they were weaving.

"One could not call them handsome," said Conán.

"One could," Fionn replied, "but it would not be true."

"I cannot see them properly," Fionn complained. "They are hiding behind the holly."

"I would be contented if I could not see them at all," his companion grumbled.

But the Chief insisted.

"I want to make sure that it is whiskers they are wearing."

"Let them wear whiskers or not wear them," Conán counselled. "But let us have nothing to do with them."

"One must not be frightened of anything," Fionn stated.

"I am not frightened," Conán explained. "I only want to keep my good opinion of women, and if the three yonder are women, then I feel sure I shall begin to dislike females from this minute out."

"Come on, my love," said Fionn, "for I must find out if these whiskers are true."

He strode resolutely into the cave. He pushed the branches of holly aside and marched up to Conaran's daughters, with Conán behind him.

Chapter 4

The instant they passed the holly a strange weakness came over the heroes. Their fists seemed to grow heavy as lead, and went dingle-dangle at the ends of their arms; their legs became as light as straws and began to bend in and out; their necks became too delicate to hold anything up, so that their heads wibbled and wobbled from side to side.

"What's wrong at all?" said Conán, as he tumbled to the ground.

"Everything is," Fionn replied, and he tumbled beside him.

The three sisters then tied the heroes with every kind of loop and twist and knot that could be thought of.

"Those are whiskers!" said Fionn.

"Alas!" said Conán.

"What a place you must hunt whiskers in!" he mumbled savagely. "Who wants whiskers?" he groaned.

But Fionn was thinking of other things.

"If there was any way of warning the Fianna not to come here," Fionn murmured.

"There is no way, my darling," said Caevóg, and she smiled a smile that would have killed Fionn, only that he shut his eyes in time.

After a moment he murmured again:

"Conán, my dear love, give the warning whistle so that the Fianna will keep out of this place."

A little whoof, like the sound that would be made by a baby and it asleep, came from Conán.

"Fionn," said he, "there isn't a whistle in me. We are done for," said he.

"You are done for, indeed," said Cuillen, and she smiled a hairy and twisty and fangy smile that almost finished Conán.

By that time some of the Fianna had returned to the mound to see why Bran and Sceólan were barking so outrageously. They saw the cave and went into it, but no sooner had they passed the holly branches than their strength went from them, and they were seized and bound by the vicious hags. Little by little all the members of the Fianna returned to the hill, and each of them was drawn into the cave, and each was bound by the sisters.

Oisín and Oscar and mac Lugac came, with the nobles of clann-Baiscne, and with those of clann-Corcoran and clann-Smól; they all came, and they were all bound.

It was a wonderful sight and a great deed this binding of the Fianna, and the three sisters laughed with a joy that was terrible to hear and was almost death to see. As the men were captured they were carried by the hags into dark mysterious holes and black perplexing labyrinths.

"Here is another one," cried Caevóg as she bundled a trussed champion along.

"This one is fat," said Cuillen, and she rolled a bulky Fenian along like a wheel.

"Here," said Iaran, "is a love of a man. One could eat this kind of man," she murmured, and she licked a lip that had whiskers growing inside as well as out.

And the corded champion whimpered in her arms, for he did not know but eating might indeed be his fate, and he would have preferred

"This one is fat," said Cuillen, and she rolled a bulky Fenian along like a wheel

to be coffined anywhere in the world rather than to be coffined inside of that face.

So far for them.

Chapter 5

Within the cave there was silence except for the voices of the hags and the scarcely audible moaning of the Fianna-Finn, but without there was a dreadful uproar, for as each man returned from the chase his dogs came with him, and although the men went into the cave the dogs did not.

They were too wise.

They stood outside, filled with savagery and terror, for they could scent their masters and their masters' danger, and perhaps they could get from the cave smells till then unknown and full of alarm.

From the troop of dogs there arose a baying and barking, a snarling and howling and growling, a yelping and squealing and bawling for which no words can be found. Now and again a dog nosed among a thousand smells and scented his master; the ruff of his neck stood up like a hog's bristles and a netty ridge prickled along his spine. Then with red eyes, with bared fangs, with a hoarse, deep snort and growl he rushed at the cave, and then he halted and sneaked back again with all his ruffles smoothed, his tail between his legs, his eyes screwed sideways in miserable apology and alarm, and a long thin whine of woe dribbling out of his nose.

The three sisters took their wide-channelled, hard-tempered swords in their hands, and prepared to slay the Fianna, but before doing so they gave one more look from the door of the cave to see if there might be a straggler of the Fianna who was escaping death by straggling, and they saw one coming towards them with Bran and

They stood outside, filled with savagery and terror

Sceólan leaping beside him, while all the other dogs began to burst their throats with barks and split their noses with snorts and wag their tails off at sight of the tall, valiant, white-toothed champion, Goll mor mac Morna.

"We will kill that one first," said Caevóg.

"There is only one of him," said Cuillen.

"And each of us three is the match for an hundred," said Iaran.

The uncanny, misbehaved, and outrageous harridans advanced then to meet the son of Morna, and when he saw these three Goll whipped the sword from his thigh, swung his buckler round, and got to them in ten great leaps.

Silence fell on the world during that conflict. The wind went down; the clouds stood still; the old hill itself held its breath; the warriors within ceased to be men and became each an ear; and the dogs sat in a vast circle round the combatants, with their heads all to one side, their noses poked forward, their mouths half open, and their tails forgotten. Now and again a dog whined in a whisper and snapped a little snap on the air, but except for that there was neither sound nor movement.

It was a long fight. It was a hard and a tricky fight, and Goll won it by bravery and strategy and great good luck; for with one shrewd slice of his blade he carved two of these mighty termagants into equal halves, so that there were noses and whiskers to his right hand and knees and toes to his left: and that stroke was known afterwards as one of the three great sword-strokes of Ireland. The third hag, however, had managed to get behind Goll, and she leaped on to his back with the bound of a panther, and hung there with the skilful, many-legged, tight-twisted clutching of a spider. But the great champion gave a twist of his hips and a swing of his shoulders that whirled her around him like a sack. He got her on the ground and tied her hands with the straps of a shield, and he was going to give her the last blow when she appealed to his honour and bravery.

"I put my life under your protection," said she. "And if you let me go free I will lift the enchantment from the Fianna-Finn and will give them all back to you again."

"I agree to that," said Goll, and he untied her straps.

The harridan did as she had promised, and in a short time Fionn and Oisín and Oscar and Conán were released, and after that all the Fianna were released.

Chapter 6

As each man came out of the cave he gave a jump and a shout; the courage of the world went into him and he felt that he could fight twenty. But while they were talking over the adventure and explaining how it had happened, a vast figure strode over the side of the hill and descended among them.

It was Conaran's fourth daughter.

If the other three had been terrible to look on, this one was more terrible than the three together. She was clad in iron plate, and she had a wicked sword by her side and a knobby club in her hand. She halted by the bodies of her sisters, and bitter tears streamed down into her beard.

"Alas, my sweet ones," said she, "I am too late."

And then she stared fiercely at Fionn.

"I demand a combat," she roared.

"It is your right," said Fionn. He turned to his son.

"Oisín, my heart, kill me this honourable hag."

But for the only time in his life Oisín shrank from a combat.

"I cannot do it" he said, "I feel too weak."

Fionn was astounded.

"Oscar," he said, "will you kill me this great hag?"

Oscar stammered miserably. "I would not be able to," he said.

Conán also refused, and so did Caelte mac Ronán and mac Lugac, for there was no man there but was terrified by the sight of that mighty and valiant harridan.

Fionn rose to his feet. "I will take this combat myself," he said sternly.

And he swung his buckler forward and stretched his right hand to the sword. But at that terrible sight Goll mae Morna blushed deeply and leaped from the ground.

"No, no," he cried; "no, my soul, Fionn, this would not be a proper combat for you. I take this fight."

"You have done your share, Goll," said the captain.

"I should finish the fight I began," Goll continued, "for it was I who killed the two sisters of this valiant hag, and it is against me the feud lies."

"That will do for me," said the horrible daughter of Conaran. "I will kill Goll mor mac Morna first, and after that I will kill Fionn, and after that I will kill every Fenian of the Fianna-Finn."

"You may begin, Goll," said Fionn, "and I give you my blessing."

Goll then strode forward to the fight, and the hag moved against him with equal alacrity. In a moment the heavens rang to the clash of swords on bucklers. It was hard to withstand the terrific blows of that mighty female, for her sword played with the quickness of lightning and smote like the heavy crashing of a storm. But into that din and encirclement Goll pressed and ventured, steady as a rock in water, agile as a creature of the sea, and when one of the combatants retreated it was the hag that gave backwards. As her foot moved a great shout of joy rose from the Fianna. A snarl went over the huge face of the monster and she leaped forward again, but she met Goll's point in the road; it went through her, and in another moment Goll took her head from its shoulders and swung it on high before Fionn.

As the Fianna turned homewards Fionn spoke to his great champion and enemy.

"Goll," he said, "I have a daughter."

"A lovely girl, a blossom of the dawn," said Goll.

"Would she please you as a wife?" the chief demanded.

"She would please me," said Goll.

"She is your wife," said Fionn.

But that did not prevent Goll from killing Fionn's brother Cairell later on, nor did it prevent Fionn from killing Goll later on again, and the last did not prevent Goll from rescuing Fionn out of hell when the Fianna-Finn were sent there under the new God. Nor is there any reason to complain or to be astonished at these things, for it is a mutual world we live in, a give-and-take world, and there is no great harm in it.

Becuma of the White Skin

Chapter 1

There are more worlds than one, and in many ways they are unlike each other. But joy and sorrow, or, in other words, good and evil, are not absent in their degree from any of the worlds, for wherever there is life there is action, and action is but the expression of one or other of these qualities.

After this Earth there is the world of the Shí. Beyond it again lies the Many-Coloured Land. Next comes the Land of Wonder, and after that the Land of Promise awaits us. You will cross clay to get into the Shí; you will cross water to attain the Many-Coloured Land; fire must be passed ere the Land of Wonder is attained, hut we do not know what will be crossed for the fourth world.

This adventure of Conn the Hundred Fighter and his son Art was by the way of water, and therefore he was more advanced in magic than Fionn was, all of whose adventures were by the path of clay and into Faery only, but Conn was the High King and so the arch-magician of Ireland.

A council had been called in the Many-Coloured Land to discuss the case of a lady named Becuma Cneisgel, that is, Becuma of the White

Skin, the daughter of Eogan Inver. She had run away from her husband Labraid and had taken refuge with Gadiar, one of the sons of Manannán mac Lir, the god of the sea, and the ruler, therefore, of that sphere.

It seems, then, that there is marriage in two other spheres. In the Shí matrimony is recorded as being parallel in every respect with earth-marriage, and the desire which urges to it seems to he as violent and inconstant as it is with us; but in the Many-Coloured Land marriage is but a contemplation of beauty, a brooding and meditation wherein all grosser desire is unknown and children are born to sinless parents.

In the Shí the crime of Becuma would have been lightly considered, and would have received none or but a nominal punishment, but in the second world a horrid gravity attaches to such a lapse, and the retribution meted is implacable and grim. It may be dissolution by fire, and that can note a destruction too final for the mind to contemplate; or it may be banishment from that sphere to a lower and worse one.

This was the fate of Becuma of the White Skin.

One may wonder how, having attained to that sphere, she could have carried with her so strong a memory of the earth. It is certain that she was not a fit person to exist in the Many-Coloured Land, and it is to be feared that she was organised too grossly even for life in the Shí.

She was an earth-woman, and she was banished to the earth.

Word was sent to the Shís of Ireland that this lady should not be permitted to enter any of them; from which it would seem that the ordinances of the Shí come from the higher world, and, it might follow, that the conduct of earth lies in the Shí.

In that way, the gates of her own world and the innumerable doors of Faery being closed against her, Becuma was forced to appear in the world of men.

It is pleasant, however, notwithstanding her terrible crime and her woeful punishment, to think how courageous she was. When she was told her sentence, nay, her doom, she made no outcry, nor did she waste any time in sorrow. She went home and put on her nicest clothes.

She wore a red satin smock, and, over this, a cloak of green silk out of which long fringes of gold swung and sparkled, and she had light sandals of white bronze on her thin, shapely feet. She had long soft hair that was yellow as gold, and soft as the curling foam of the sea. Her eyes were wide and clear as water and were grey as a dove's breast. Her teeth were white as snow and of an evenness to marvel at. Her lips were thin and beautifully curved: red lips in truth, red as winter berries and tempting as the fruits of summer. The people who superintended her departure said mournfully that when she was gone there would be no more beauty left in their world.

She stepped into a coracle, it was pushed on the enchanted waters, and it went forward, world within world, until land appeared, and her boat swung in low tide against a rock at the foot of Ben Edair.

So far for her.

Chapter 2

Conn the Hundred Fighter, Ard-Rí of Ireland, was in the lowest spirits that can be imagined, for his wife was dead. He had been Ard-Rí for nine years, and during his term the corn used to be reaped three times in each year, and there was full and plenty of everything. There are few kings who can boast of more kingly results than he can, but there was sore trouble in store for him.

He had been married to Eithne, the daughter of Brisland Binn, King of Norway, and, next to his subjects, he loved his wife more than all that was lovable in the world. But the term of man and woman, of king or queen, is set in the stars, and there is no escaping Doom for any one; so, when her time came, Eithne died.

Now there were three great burying-places in Ireland—the Brugh of the Boyne in Ulster, over which Angus Og is chief and god; the Shí mound of Cruachan Ahi, where Ethal Anbual presides over the underworld of Connacht; and Tailltin, in Royal Meath. It was in this last, the sacred place of his own lordship, that Conn laid his wife to rest.

Her funeral games were played during nine days. Her keen was sung by poets and harpers, and a cairn ten acres wide was heaved over her clay. Then the keening ceased and the games drew to an end; the princes of the Five Provinces returned by horse or by chariot to their own places; the concourse of mourners melted away, and there was nothing left by the great cairn but the sun that dozed upon it in the daytime, the heavy clouds that brooded on it in the night, and the desolate, memoried king.

For the dead queen had been so lovely that Conn could not forget her; she had been so kind at every moment that he could not but miss her at every moment; but it was in the Council Chamber and the Judgement Hall that he most pondered her memory. For she had also been wise, and lacking her guidance, all grave affairs seemed graver, shadowing each day and going with him to the pillow at night.

The trouble of the king becomes the trouble of the subject, for how shall we live if judgement is withheld, or if faulty decisions are promulgated? Therefore, with the sorrow of the king, all Ireland was in grief, and it was the wish of every person that he should marry again.

Such an idea, however, did not occur to him, for he could not conceive how any woman should fill the place his queen had vacated. He grew more and more despondent, and less and less fitted to cope with affairs of state, and one day he instructed his son Art to take the rule during his absence, and he set out for Ben Edair.

For a great wish had come upon him to walk beside the sea; to listen to the roll and boom of long, grey breakers; to gaze on an unfruitful, desolate wilderness of waters; and to forget in those sights all that he could forget, and if he could not forget then to remember all that he should remember.

He was thus gazing and brooding when one day he observed a coracle drawing to the shore. A young girl stepped from it and walked to him among black boulders and patches of yellow sand.

Chapter 3

Being a king he had authority to ask questions. Conn asked her, therefore, all the questions that he could think of, for it is not every day that a lady drives from the sea, and she wearing a golden-fringed cloak of green silk through which a red satin smock peeped at the openings. She replied to his questions, but she did not tell him all the truth; for, indeed, she could not afford to.

She knew who he was, for she retained some of the powers proper to the worlds she had left, and as he looked on her soft yellow hair and on her thin red lips, Conn recognised, as all men do, that one who is lovely must also be good, and so he did not frame any inquiry on that count; for everything is forgotten in the presence of a pretty woman, and a magician can be bewitched also.

She told Conn that the fame of his son Art had reached even the Many-Coloured Land, and that she had fallen in love with the boy. This did not seem unreasonable to one who had himself ventured much in Faery, and who had known so many of the people of that world leave their own land for the love of a mortal.

"What is your name, my sweet lady?" said the king.

"I am called Delvcaem (Fair Shape) and I am the daughter of Morgan," she replied.

"I have heard much of Morgan," said the king. "He is a very great magician."

During this conversation Conn had been regarding her with the minute freedom which is right only in a king. At what precise instant he forgot his dead consort we do not know, but it is certain that at this moment his mind was no longer burdened with that dear and lovely memory. His voice was melancholy when he spoke again.

"You love my son!"

"Who could avoid loving him?" she murmured.

"When a woman speaks to a man about the love she feels for another man she is not liked. And," he continued, "when she speaks to a man who has no wife of his own about her love for another man then she is disliked."

"I would not be disliked by you," Becuma murmured.

"Nevertheless," said he regally, "I will not come between a woman and her choice."

"I did not know you lacked a wife," said Becuma, but indeed she did.

"You know it now," the king replied sternly.

"What shall I do?" she inquired, "am I to wed you or your son?"

"You must choose," Conn answered.

"If you allow me to choose it means that you do not want me very badly," said she with a smile.

"Then I will not allow you to choose," cried the king, "and it is with myself you shall marry."

He took her hand in his and kissed it.

"Lovely is this pale thin hand. Lovely is the slender foot that I see in a small bronze shoe," said the king.

After a suitable time she continued:

"I should not like your son to be at Tara when I am there, or for a year afterwards, for I do not wish to meet him until I have forgotten him and have come to know you well."

"I do not wish to banish my son," the king protested.

"It would not really be a banishment," she said. "A prince's duty could be set him, and in such an absence he would improve his knowledge both of Ireland and of men. Further," she continued with downcast eyes, "when you remember the reason that brought me here you will see that his presence would be an embarrassment to us both, and my presence would be unpleasant to him if he remembers his mother."

"Nevertheless," said Conn stubbornly, "I do not wish to banish my son; it is awkward and unnecessary."

"For a year only," she pleaded.

"It is yet," he continued thoughtfully, "a reasonable reason that you give and I will do what you ask, but by my hand and word I don't like doing it."

They set out then briskly and joyfully on the homeward journey, and in due time they reached Tara of the Kings.

Chapter 4

It is part of the education of a prince to be a good chess player, and to continually exercise his mind in view of the judgements that he will be called upon to give and the knotty, tortuous, and perplexing matters which will obscure the issues which he must judge. Art, the son of Conn, was sitting at chess with Cromdes, his father's magician.

"Be very careful about the move you are going to make," said Cromdes.

"*Can* I be careful?" Art inquired. "Is the move that you are thinking of in my power?"

"It is not," the other admitted.

"Then I need not be more careful than usual," Art replied, and he made his move.

"It is a move of banishment," said Cromdes.

"As I will not banish myself, I suppose my father will do it, but I do not know why he should."

"Your father will not banish you."

"Who then?"

"Your mother."

"My mother is dead."

"You have a new one," said the magician.

"Here is news," said Art. "I think I shall not love my new mother."

"You will yet love her better than she loves you," said Cromdes, meaning thereby that they would hate each other.

While they spoke the king and Becuma entered the palace.

"I had better go to greet my father," said the young man.

"You had better wait until he sends for you," his companion advised, and they returned to their game.

In due time a messenger came from the king directing Art to leave Tara instantly, and to leave Ireland for one full year.

He left Tara that night, and for the space of a year he was not seen again in Ireland. But during that period things did not go well with the king nor with Ireland. Every year before that time three crops of corn used to be lifted off the land, but during Art's absence there was no corn in Ireland and there was no milk. The whole land went hungry.

Lean people were in every house, lean cattle in every field; the bushes did not swing out their timely berries or seasonable nuts; the bees went abroad as busily as ever, but each night they returned languidly, with empty pouches, and there was no honey in their hives when the honey season came. People began to look at each other questioningly, meaningly, and dark remarks passed between them, for they knew that a bad harvest means, somehow, a bad king, and, although this belief can be combated, it is too firmly rooted in wisdom to be dismissed.

The poets and magicians met to consider why this disaster should have befallen the country and by their arts they discovered the truth about the king's wife, and that she was Becuma of the White Skin, and they discovered also the cause of her banishment from the Many-Coloured Land that is beyond the sea, which is beyond even the grave.

They told the truth to the king, but he could not bear to be parted from that slender-handed, gold-haired, thin-lipped, blithe enchantress, and he required them to discover some means whereby he might retain his wife and his crown. There was a way and the magicians told him of it.

"If the son of a sinless couple can be found and if his blood be mixed with the soil of Tara the blight and ruin will depart from Ireland," said the magicians.

"If there is such a boy I will find him," cried the Hundred Fighter.

At the end of a year Art returned to Tara. His father delivered to him the sceptre of Ireland, and he set out on a journey to find the son of a sinless couple such as he had been told of.

Chapter 5

The High King did not know where exactly he should look for such a saviour, but he was well educated and knew how to look for whatever was lacking. This knowledge will be useful to those upon whom a similar duty should ever devolve.

He went to Ben Edair. He stepped into a coracle and pushed out to the deep, and he permitted the coracle to go as the winds and the waves directed it.

In such a way he voyaged among the small islands of the sea until he lost all knowledge of his course and was adrift far out in ocean. He was under the guidance of the stars and the great luminaries.

He saw black seals that stared and barked and dived dancingly, with the round turn of a bow and the forward onset of an arrow. Great whales came heaving from the green-hued void, blowing a wave of the sea high into the air from their noses and smacking their wide flat tails thunderously on the water. Porpoises went snorting past in bands and clans. Small fish came sliding and flickering, and all the outlandish creatures of the deep rose by his bobbing craft and swirled and sped away.

Wild storms howled by him so that the boat climbed painfully to the sky on a mile-high wave, balanced for a tense moment on its level top, and sped down the glassy side as a stone goes furiously from a sling.

Or, again, caught in the chop of a broken sea, it stayed shuddering and backing, while above his head there was only a low sad sky, and around him the lap and wash of grey waves that were never the same and were never different.

After long staring on the hungry nothingness of air and water he would stare on the skin-stretched fabric of his boat as on a strangeness, or he would examine his hands and the texture of his skin and the stiff black hairs that grew behind his knuckles and sprouted around his ring, and he found in these things newness and wonder.

Then, when days of storm had passed, the low grey clouds shivered and cracked in a thousand places, each grim islet went scudding to the horizon as though terrified by some great breadth, and when they had passed he stared into vast after vast of blue infinity, in the depths of which his eyes stayed and could not pierce, and wherefrom they could scarcely be withdrawn. A sun beamed thence that filled the air with sparkle and the sea with a thousand lights, and looking on these he was reminded of his home at Tara: of the columns of white and yellow bronze that blazed out sunnily on the sun, and the red and white and yellow painted roofs that beamed at and astonished the eye.

Sailing thus, lost in a succession of days and nights, of winds and calms, he came at last to an island.

His back was turned to it, and long before he saw it he smelled it and wondered; for he had been sitting as in a daze, musing on a change

that had seemed to come in his changeless world; and for a long time he could not tell what that was which made a difference on the salt-whipped wind or why he should be excited. For suddenly he had become excited and his heart leaped in violent expectation.

"It is an October smell," he said.

"It is apples that I smell."

He turned then and saw the island, fragrant with apple trees, sweet with wells of wine; and, hearkening towards the shore, his ears, dulled yet with the unending rhythms of the sea, distinguished and were filled with song; for the isle was, as it were, a nest of birds, and they sang joyously, sweetly, triumphantly.

He landed on that lovely island, and went forward under the darting birds, under the apple boughs, skirting fragrant lakes about which were woods of the sacred hazel and into which the nuts of knowledge fell and swam; and he blessed the gods of his people because of the ground that did not shiver and because of the deeply rooted trees that could not gad or budge.

Chapter 6

Having gone some distance by these pleasant ways he saw a shapely house dozing in the sunlight.

It was thatched with the wings of birds, blue wings and yellow and white wings, and in the centre of the house there was a door of crystal set in posts of bronze.

The queen of this island lived there, Rigru (Large-eyed), the daughter of Lodan, and wife of Daire Degamra. She was seated on a crystal throne with her son Segda by her side, and they welcomed the High King courteously.

There were no servants in this palace; nor was there need for them.

The High King found that his hands had washed themselves, and when later on he noticed that food had been placed before him he noticed also that it had come without the assistance of servile hands. A cloak was laid gently about his shoulders, and he was glad of it, for his own was soiled by exposure to sun and wind and water, and was not worthy of a lady's eye.

Then he was invited to eat.

He noticed, however, that food had been set for no one but himself, and this did not please him, for to eat alone was contrary to the hospitable usage of a king, and was contrary also to his contract with the gods.

"Good, my hosts," he remonstrated, "it is geasa (taboo) for me to eat alone."

"But we never eat together," the queen replied.

"I cannot violate my geasa," said the High King.

"I will eat with you," said Segda (Sweet Speech), "and thus, while you are our guest you will not do violence to your vows."

"Indeed," said Conn, "that will be a great satisfaction, for I have already all the trouble that I can cope with and have no wish to add to it by offending the gods."

"What is your trouble?" the gentle queen asked.

"During a year," Conn replied, "there has been neither corn nor milk in Ireland. The land is parched, the trees are withered, the birds do not sing in Ireland, and the bees do not make honey."

"You are certainly in trouble," the queen assented.

"But," she continued, "for what purpose have you come to our island?"

"I have come to ask for the loan of your son."

"A loan of my son!"

"I have been informed," Conn explained, "that if the son of a sinless couple is brought to Tara and is bathed in the waters of Ireland the land will be delivered from those ills."

The king of this island, Daire, had not hitherto spoken, but he now did so with astonishment and emphasis.

"We would not lend our son to any one, not even to gain the kingship of the world," said he.

But Segda, observing that the guest's countenance was discomposed, broke in:

"It is not kind to refuse a thing that the Ard-Rí of Ireland asks for, and I will go with him."

"Do not go, my pulse," his father advised.

"Do not go, my one treasure," his mother pleaded.

"I must go indeed," the boy replied, "for it is to do good I am required, and no person may shirk such a requirement."

"Go then," said his father, "but I will place you under the protection of the High King and of the Four Provincial Kings of Ireland, and under the protection of Art, the son of Conn, and of Fionn, the son of Uail, and under the protection of the magicians and poets and the men of art in Ireland." And he thereupon bound these protections and safeguards on the Ard-Rí with an oath.

"I will answer for these protections," said Conn.

He departed then from the island with Segda and in three days they reached Ireland, and in due time they arrived at Tara.

Chapter 7

On reaching the palace Conn called his magicians and poets to a council and informed them that he had found the boy they sought—the son of a virgin. These learned people consulted together, and they stated that the young man must be killed, and that his blood should be mixed with the earth of Tara and sprinkled under the withered trees.

When Segda heard this he was astonished and defiant; then, seeing that he was alone and without prospect of succour, he grew downcast and was in great fear for his life. But remembering the safeguards under which he had been placed, he enumerated these to the assembly, and called on the High King to grant him the protections that were his due.

Conn was greatly perturbed, but, as in duty bound, he placed the boy under the various protections that were in his oath, and, with the courage of one who has no more to gain or lose, he placed Segda, furthermore, under the protection of all the men of Ireland.

But the men of Ireland refused to accept that bond, saying that although the Ard-Rí was acting justly towards the boy he was not acting justly towards Ireland.

"We do not wish to slay this prince for our pleasure," they argued, "but for the safety of Ireland he must be killed."

Angry parties were formed. Art, and Fionn the son of Uail, and the princes of the land were outraged at the idea that one who had been placed under their protection should be hurt by any hand. But the men of Ireland and the magicians stated that the king had gone to Faery for a special purpose, and that his acts outside or contrary to that purpose were illegal, and committed no person to obedience.

There were debates in the Council Hall, in the market-place, in the streets of Tara, some holding that national honour dissolved and absolved all personal honour, and others protesting that no man had aught but his personal honour, and that above it not the gods, not even Ireland, could be placed—for it is to be known that Ireland is a god.

Such a debate was in course, and Segda, to whom both sides addressed gentle and courteous arguments, grew more and more disconsolate.

"You shall die for Ireland, dear heart," said one of them, and he gave Segda three kisses on each cheek.

"Indeed," said Segda, returning those kisses, "indeed I had not bargained to die for Ireland, but only to bathe in her waters and to remove her pestilence."

"But dear child and prince," said another, kissing him likewise, "if any one of us could save Ireland by dying for her how cheerfully we would die."

And Segda, returning his three kisses, agreed that the death was noble, but that it was not in his undertaking.

Then, observing the stricken countenances about him, and the faces of men and women hewn thin by hunger, his resolution melted away, and he said:

"I think I must die for you," and then he said:

"I will die for you."

And when he had said that, all the people present touched his cheek with their lips, and the love and peace of Ireland entered into his soul, so that he was tranquil and proud and happy.

The executioner drew his wide, thin blade and all those present covered their eyes with their cloaks, when a wailing voice called on the executioner to delay yet a moment. The High King uncovered his eyes and saw that a woman had approached driving a cow before her.

"Why are you killing the boy?" she demanded.

The reason for this slaying was explained to her.

"Are you sure," she asked, "that the poets and magicians really know everything?"

"Do they not?" the king inquired.

"Do they?" she insisted.

And then turning to the magicians:

"Let one magician of the magicians tell me what is hidden in the bags that are lying across the back of my cow."

But no magician could tell it, nor did they try to.

"Questions are not answered thus," they said. "There is formulae, and the calling up of spirits, and lengthy complicated preparations in our art."

"I am not badly learned in these arts," said the woman, "and I say that if you slay this cow the effect will be the same as if you had killed the boy."

"We would prefer to kill a cow or a thousand cows rather than harm this young prince," said Conn, "but if we spare the boy will these evils return?"

"They will not be banished until you have banished their cause."

"And what is their cause?"

"Becuma is the cause, and she must be banished."

"If you must tell me what to do," said Conn, "tell me at least to do something that I can do."

"I will tell you certainly. You can keep Becuma and your ills as long as you want to. It does not matter to me. Come, my son," she said to Segda, for it was Segda's mother who had come to save him; and then that sinless queen and her son went back to their home of enchantment, leaving the king and Fionn and the magicians and nobles of Ireland astonished and ashamed.

Chapter 8

There are good and evil people in this and in every other world, and the person who goes hence will go to the good or the evil that is native to him, while those who return come as surely to their due. The trouble which had fallen on Becuma did not leave her repentant, and the sweet lady began to do wrong as instantly and innocently as a flower begins to grow. It was she who was responsible for the ills which had come on Ireland, and we may wonder why she brought these plagues and droughts to what was now her own country.

Under all wrong-doing lies personal vanity or the feeling that we are endowed and privileged beyond our fellows. It is probable that, however courageously she had accepted fate, Becuma had been sharply stricken in her pride; in the sense of personal strength, aloofness, and identity, in which the mind likens itself to god and will resist every domination but its own. She had been punished, that is, she had submitted to control, and her sense of freedom, of privilege, of very being, was outraged. The mind flinches even from the control of natural law, and how much more from the despotism of its own separated likenesses, for if another can control me that other has usurped me, has become me, and how terribly I seem diminished by the seeming addition!

This sense of separateness is vanity, and is the bed of all wrong-doing. For we are not freedom, we are control, and we must submit to our own function ere we can exercise it. Even unconsciously we accept the rights of others to all that we have, and if we will not share our good with them, it is because we cannot, having none; but we will yet give what we have, although that be evil. To insist on other people sharing in our personal torment is the first step towards insisting that they shall share in our joy, as we shall insist when we get it.

Becuma considered that if she must suffer all else she met should suffer also. She raged, therefore, against Ireland, and in particular she raged against young Art, her husband's son, and she left undone nothing that could afflict Ireland or the prince. She may have felt that she could not make them suffer, and that is a maddening thought to any woman. Or perhaps she had really desired the son instead of the father, and her thwarted desire had perpetuated itself as hate. But it is true that Art regarded his mother's successor with intense dislike, and it is true that she actively returned it.

One day Becuma came on the lawn before the palace, and seeing that Art was at chess with Cromdes she walked to the table on which the match was being played and for some time regarded the game. But the young prince did not take any notice of her while she stood by the board, for he knew that this girl was the enemy of Ireland, and he could not bring himself even to look at her.

Becuma, looking down on his beautiful head, smiled as much in rage as in disdain.

"O son of a king," said she, "I demand a game with you for stakes."

Art then raised his head and stood up courteously, but he did not look at her.

"Whatever the queen demands I will do," said he.

"Am I not your mother also?" she replied mockingly, as she took the seat which the chief magician leaped from.

The game was set then, and her play was so skilful that Art was hard put to counter her moves. But at a point of the game Becuma grew thoughtful, and, as by a lapse of memory, she made a move which gave the victory to her opponent. But she had intended that. She sat then, biting on her lip with her white small teeth and staring angrily at Art.

"What do you demand from me?" she asked.

"I bind you to eat no food in Ireland until you find the wand of Curoi, son of Darè."

Becuma then put a cloak about her and she went from Tara northward and eastward until she came to the dewy, sparkling Brugh of Angus mac an Og in Ulster, but she was not admitted there. She went thence to the Shí ruled over by Eogabal, and although this lord would not admit her, his daughter Ainè, who was her foster-sister, let her into Faery. She made inquiries and was informed where the dun of Curoi mac Darè was, and when she had received this intelligence she set out for Sliev Mis. By what arts she coaxed Curoi to give up his wand it matters not, enough that she was able to return in triumph to Tara. When she handed the wand to Art, she said:

"I claim my game of revenge."

"It is due to you," said Art, and they sat on the lawn before the palace and played.

A hard game that was, and at times each of the combatants sat for an hour staring on the board before the next move was made, and at times they looked from the board and for hours stared on the sky seeking as though in heaven for advice. But Becuma's foster-sister, Ainè, came from the Shí, and, unseen by any, she interfered with Art's play, so that, suddenly, when he looked again on the board, his face went pale, for he saw that the game was lost.

"I didn't move that piece," said he sternly.

"Nor did I," Becuma replied, and she called on the onlookers to confirm that statement.

She was smiling to herself secretly, for she had seen what the mortal eyes around could not see.

"I think the game is mine," she insisted softly.

"I think that your friends in Faery have cheated," he replied, "but the game is yours if you are content to win it that way."

"I bind you," said Becuma, "to eat no food in Ireland until you have found Delvcaem, the daughter of Morgan."

"Where do I look for her?" said Art in despair.

"She is in one of the islands of the sea," Becuma replied, "that is all I will tell you," and she looked at him maliciously, joyously, contentedly, for she thought he would never return from that journey, and that Morgan would see to it.

Chapter 9

Art, as his father had done before him, set out for the Many-Coloured Land, but it was from Inver Colpa he embarked and not from Ben Edair.

At a certain time he passed from the rough green ridges of the sea to enchanted waters, and he roamed from island to island asking all people how he might come to Delvcaem, the daughter of Morgan. But he got no news from any one, until he reached an island that was fragrant with wild apples, gay with flowers, and joyous with the song of birds and the deep mellow drumming of the bees. In this island he was met by a lady, Credè, the Truly Beautiful, and when they had exchanged kisses, he told her who he was and on what errand he was bent.

"We have been expecting you," said Credè, "but alas, poor soul, it is a hard, and a long, bad way that you must go; for there is sea and land, danger and difficulty between you and the daughter of Morgan."

"Yet I must go there," he answered.

"There is a wild dark ocean to be crossed. There is a dense wood where every thorn on every tree is sharp as a spear-point and is curved and clutching. There is a deep gulf to be gone through," she said, "a place of silence and terror, full of dumb, venomous monsters. There is an immense oak forest—dark, dense, thorny, a place to be strayed in, a place to be utterly bewildered and lost in. There is a vast dark wilderness, and therein is a dark house, lonely and full of echoes, and in it there are seven gloomy hags, who are warned already of your coming and are waiting to plunge you in a bath of molten lead."

"It is not a choice journey," said Art, "but I have no choice and must go."

"Should you pass those hags," she continued, "and no one has yet passed them, you must meet Ailill of the Black Teeth, the son of Mongan Tender Blossom, and who could pass that gigantic and terrible fighter?"

"It is not easy to find the daughter of Morgan," said Art in a melancholy voice.

"It is not easy," Credè replied eagerly, "and if you will take my advice—"

"Advise me," he broke in, "for in truth there is no man standing in such need of counsel as I do."

"I would advise you," said Credè in a low voice, "to seek no more for the sweet daughter of Morgan, but to stay in this place where all that is lovely is at your service."

"But, but—" cried Art in astonishment.

"Am I not as sweet as the daughter of Morgan?" she demanded, and she stood before him queenly and pleadingly, and her eyes took his with imperious tenderness.

"By my hand," he answered, "you are sweeter and lovelier than any being under the sun, but—"

"And with me," she said, "you will forget Ireland."

"I am under bonds," cried Art, "I have passed my word, and I would not forget Ireland or cut myself from it for all the kingdoms of the Many-Coloured Land."

Credè urged no more at that time, but as they were parting she whispered, "There are two girls, sisters of my own, in Morgan's palace. They will come to you with a cup in either hand; one cup will be filled with wine and one with poison. Drink from the right-hand cup, O my dear."

Art stepped into his coracle, and then, wringing her hands, she made yet an attempt to dissuade him from that drear journey.

"Do not leave me," she urged. "Do not affront these dangers. Around the palace of Morgan there is a palisade of copper spikes, and on the top of each spike the head of a man grins and shrivels. There is one spike only which bears no head, and it is for your head that spike is waiting. Do not go there, my love."

"I must go indeed," said Art earnestly.

"There is yet a danger," she called. "Beware of Delvcaem's mother, Dog Head, daughter of the King of the Dog Heads. Beware of her."

"Indeed," said Art to himself, "there is so much to beware of that I will beware of nothing. I will go about my business," he said to the waves, "and I will let those beings and monsters and the people of the Dog Heads go about their business."

Chapter 10

He went forward in his light bark, and at some moment found that he had parted from those seas and was adrift on vaster and more turbulent billows. From those dark-green surges there gaped at him monstrous and cavernous jaws; and round, wicked, red-rimmed, bulging eyes stared fixedly at the boat. A ridge of inky water rushed foaming mountainously on his board, and behind that ridge came a vast warty head that gurgled and groaned. But at these vile creatures he thrust with his lengthy spear or stabbed at closer reach with a dagger.

He was not spared one of the terrors which had been foretold. Thus, in the dark thick oak forest he slew the seven hags and buried them in the molten lead which they had heated for him. He climbed an icy mountain, the cold breath of which seemed to slip into his body and chip off inside of his bones, and there, until he mastered the sort of climbing on ice, for each step that he took upwards he slipped back ten steps. Almost his heart gave way before he learned to climb that venomous hill. In a forked glen into which he slipped at night-fall he was surrounded by giant toads, who spat poison, and were icy as the land they lived in, and were cold and foul and savage. At Sliav Saev he encountered the long-maned lions who lie in wait for the beasts of the world, growling woefully as they squat above their prey and crunch those terrified bones. He came on Ailill of the Black Teeth sitting on the bridge that spanned a torrent, and the grim giant was grinding his teeth on a pillar stone. Art drew nigh unobserved and brought him low.

It was not for nothing that these difficulties and dangers were in his path. These things and creatures were the invention of Dog Head, the wife of Morgan, for it had become known to her that she would die on the day her daughter was wooed. Therefore none of the dangers encountered by Art were real, but were magical chimeras conjured against him by the great witch.

Affronting all, conquering all, he came in time to Morgan's dun, a place so lovely that after the miseries through which he had struggled he almost wept to see beauty again.

Delvcaem knew that he was coming. She was waiting for him, yearning for him. To her mind Art was not only love, he was freedom, for the poor girl was a captive in her father's home. A great pillar an hundred feet high had been built on the roof of Morgan's palace, and on the top of this pillar a tiny room had been constructed, and in this room Delvcaem was a prisoner.

She was lovelier in shape than any other princess of the Many-Coloured Land. She was wiser than all the other women of that land, and she was skilful in music, embroidery, and chastity, and in all else that pertained to the knowledge of a queen.

Although Delvcaem's mother wished nothing but ill to Art, she yet treated him with the courtesy proper in a queen on the one hand and fitting towards the son of the King of Ireland on the other. Therefore, when Art entered the palace he was met and kissed, and he was bathed and clothed and fed. Two young girls came to him then, having a cup in each of their hands, and presented him with the kingly drink, but, remembering the warning which Credè had given him, he drank only from the right-hand cup and escaped the poison.

Next he was visited by Delvcaem's mother, Dog Head, daughter of the King of the Dog Heads, and Morgan's queen. She was dressed in full armour, and she challenged Art to fight with her.

It was a woeful combat, for there was no craft or sagacity unknown to her, and Art would infallibly have perished by her hand but that her days were numbered, her star was out, and her time had come. It was her head that rolled on the ground when the combat was over, and it was her head that grinned and shrivelled on the vacant spike which she had reserved for Art's.

Then Art liberated Delvcaem from her prison at the top of the pillar and they were affianced together. But the ceremony had scarcely been completed when the tread of a single man caused the palace to quake and seemed to jar the world.

It was Morgan returning to the palace.

The gloomy king challenged him to combat also, and in his honour Art put on the battle harness which he had brought from Ireland. He wore a breastplate and helmet of gold, a mantle of blue satin swung from his shoulders, his left hand was thrust into the grips of a purple shield, deeply bossed with silver, and in the other hand he held the wide-grooved, blue hilted sword which had rung so often into fights and combats, and joyous feats and exercises.

Up to this time the trials through which he had passed had seemed so great that they could not easily be added to. But if all those trials had been gathered into one vast calamity they would not equal one half of the rage and catastrophe of his war with Morgan.

For what he could not effect by arms Morgan would endeavour by guile, so that while Art drove at him or parried a crafty blow, the shape of Morgan changed before his eyes, and the monstrous king was having at him in another form, and from a new direction.

It was well for the son of the Ard-Rí that he had been beloved by the poets and magicians of his land, and that they had taught him all that was known of shape-changing and words of power.

He had need of all these.

At times, for the weapon must change with the enemy, they fought with their foreheads as two giant stags, and the crash of their monstrous onslaught rolled and lingered on the air long after their skulls had parted. Then as two lions, long-clawed, deep-mouthed, snarling, with rigid mane, with red-eyed glare, with flashing, sharp-white fangs, they prowled lithely about each other seeking for an opening. And then as two green-ridged, white-topped, broad-swung, overwhelming, vehement billows of the deep, they met and crashed and sunk into and rolled away from each other; and the noise of these two waves was as the roar of all ocean when the howl of the tempest is drowned in the league-long fury of the surge.

But when the wife's time has come the husband is doomed. He is required elsewhere by his beloved, and Morgan went to rejoin his queen in the world that comes after the Many-Coloured Land, and his victor shore that knowledgeable head away from its giant shoulders.

The waves of all the worlds seemed to whirl past them in one huge green cataract

He did not tarry in the Many-Coloured Land, for he had nothing further to seek there. He gathered the things which pleased him best from among the treasures of its grisly king, and with Delvcaem by his side they stepped into the coracle.

Then, setting their minds on Ireland, they went there as it were in a flash.

The waves of all the world seemed to whirl past them in one huge, green cataract. The sound of all these oceans boomed in their ears for one eternal instant. Nothing was for that moment but a vast roar and pour of waters. Thence they swung into a silence equally vast, and so sudden that it was as thunderous in the comparison as was the elemental rage they quitted. For a time they sat panting, staring at each other, holding each other, lest not only their lives but their very souls should be swirled away in the gusty passage of world within world; and then, looking abroad, they saw the small bright waves creaming by the rocks of Ben Edair, and they blessed the power that had guided and protected them, and they blessed the comely land of Ir.

On reaching Tara, Delvcaem, who was more powerful in art and magic than Becuma, ordered the latter to go away, and she did so.

She left the king's side. She came from the midst of the counsellors and magicians. She did not bid farewell to any one. She did not say good-bye to the king as she set out for Ben Edair.

Where she could go to no man knew, for she had been banished from the Many-Coloured Land and could not return there. She was forbidden entry to the Shí by Angus Og, and she could not remain in Ireland. She went to Sasana and she became a queen in that country, and it was she who fostered the rage against the Holy Land which has not ceased to this day.

Mongan's Frenzy

Chapter 1

The abbot of the Monastery of Moville sent word to the story-tellers of Ireland that when they were in his neighbourhood they should call at the monastery, for he wished to collect and write down the stories which were in danger of being forgotten.

"These things also must he told," said he.

In particular he wished to gather tales which told of the deeds that had been done before the Gospel came to Ireland.

"For," said he, "there are very good tales among those ones, and it would be a pity if the people who come after us should be ignorant of what happened long ago, and of the deeds of their fathers."

So, whenever a story-teller chanced in that neighbourhood he was directed to the monastery, and there he received a welcome and his fill of all that is good for man.

The abbot's manuscript boxes began to fill up, and he used to regard that growing store with pride and joy. In the evenings, when the days grew short and the light went early, he would call for some one of these manuscripts and have it read to him by candle-light, in order that he might satisfy himself that it was as good as he had judged it to be on the previous hearing.

One day a story-teller came to the monastery, and, like all the others, he was heartily welcomed and given a great deal more than his need.

He said that his name was Cairidè, and that he had a story to tell which could not be bettered among the stories of Ireland.

The abbot's eyes glistened when he heard that. He rubbed his hands together and smiled on his guest.

"What is the name of your story?" he asked.

"It is called 'Mongan's Frenzy.' "

"I never heard of it before," cried the abbot joyfully.

"I am the only man that knows it," Cairidè replied.

"But how does that come about?" the abbot inquired.

"Because it belongs to my family," the story-teller answered. "There was a Cairidè of my nation with Mongan when he went into Faery. This Cairidè listened to the story when it was first told. Then he told it to his son, and his son told it to his son, and that son's great-great-grandson's son told it to his son's son, and he told it to my father, and my father told it to me."

"And you shall tell it to me," cried the abbot triumphantly.

"I will indeed," said Cairidè.

Vellum was then brought and quills. The copyists sat at their tables. Ale was placed beside the story-teller, and he told this tale to the abbot.

Chapter 2

Said Cairidè:

Mongan's wife at that time was Brótiarna, the Flame Lady. She was passionate and fierce, and because the blood would flood suddenly to her cheek, so that she who had seemed a lily became, while you looked upon her, a rose, she was called Flame Lady. She loved Mongan with ecstasy and abandon, and for that also he called her Flame Lady.

But there may have been something of calculation even in her wildest moment, for if she was delighted in her affection she was tormented in it also, as are all those who love the great ones of life and strive to equal themselves where equality is not possible.

For her husband was at once more than himself and less than himself. He was less than himself because he was now Mongan. He was more than himself because he was one who had long disappeared from the world of men. His lament had been sung and his funeral games played many, many years before, and Brótiarna sensed in him secrets, experiences, knowledges in which she could have no part, and for which she was greedily envious.

So she was continually asking him little, simple questions à propos of every kind of thing.

She weighed all that he said on whatever subject, and when he talked in his sleep she listened to his dream.

The knowledge that she gleaned from those listenings tormented her far more than it satisfied her, for the names of other women were continually on his lips, sometimes in terms of dear affection, sometimes in accents of anger or despair, and in his sleep he spoke familiarly of people whom the story-tellers told of, but who had been dead for centuries. Therefore she was perplexed, and became filled with a very rage of curiosity.

Among the names which her husband mentioned there was one which, because of the frequency with which it appeared, and because of the tone of anguish and love and longing in which it was uttered, she thought of oftener than the others: this name was Duv Laca. Although she questioned and cross-questioned Cairidè, her story-teller, she could discover nothing about a lady who had been known as the Black Duck. But one night when Mongan seemed to speak with Duv Laca he mentioned her father as Fiachna Duv mac Demain, and the story-teller said that king had been dead for a vast number of years.

She asked her husband then, boldly, to tell her the story of Duv Laca, and under the influence of their mutual love he promised to tell it to her some time, but each time she reminded him of his promise he became confused, and said that he would tell it some other time.

As time went on the poor Flame Lady grew more and more jealous of Duv Laca, and more and more certain that, if only she could know what had happened, she would get some ease to her tormented heart and some assuagement of her perfectly natural curiosity. Therefore she lost no opportunity of reminding Mongan of his promise, and on each occasion he renewed the promise and put it back to another time.

Chapter 3

In the year when Ciaran the son of the Carpenter died, the same year when Tuathal Maelgariv was killed and the year when Diarmait the son of Cerrbel became king of all Ireland, the year 538 of our era in short, it happened that there was a great gathering of the men of Ireland at the Hill of Uisneach in Royal Meath.

In addition to the Council which was being held, there were games and tournaments and brilliant deployments of troops, and universal feastings and enjoyments. The gathering lasted for a week, and on the last day of the week Mongan was moving through the crowd with seven guards, his story-teller Cairidè, and his wife.

It had been a beautiful day, with brilliant sunshine and great sport, but suddenly clouds began to gather in the sky to the west, and others came rushing blackly from the east. When these clouds met the world went dark for a space, and there fell from the sky a shower of hailstones, so large that each man wondered at their size, and so swift and heavy that the women and young people of the host screamed from the pain of the blows they received.

Mongan's men made a roof of their shields, and the hailstones battered on the shields so terribly that even under them they were afraid. They began to move away from the host looking for shelter, and when they had gone apart a little way they turned the edge of a small hill and a knoll of trees, and in the twinkling of an eye they were in fair weather.

One minute they heard the clashing and bashing of the hailstones, the howling of the venomous wind, the screams of women and the uproar of the crowd on the Hill of Uisneach, and the next minute they heard nothing more of those sounds and saw nothing more of these sights, for they had been permitted to go at one step out of the world of men and into the world of Faery.

Chapter 4

There is a difference between this world and the world of Faery, but it is not immediately perceptible. Everything that is here is there, but the things that are there are better than those that are here. All things that are bright are there brighter. There is more gold in the sun and more silver in the moon of that land. There is more scent in the flowers, more savour in the fruit. There is more comeliness in the men and more tenderness in the women. Everything in Faery is better by this one wonderful degree, and it is by this betterness you will know that you are there if you should ever happen to get there.

Mongan and his companions stepped from the world of storm into sunshine and a scented world. The instant they stepped they stood, bewildered, looking at each other silently, questioningly, and then with one accord they turned to look back whence they had come.

There was no storm behind them. The sunlight drowsed there as it did in front, a peaceful flooding of living gold. They saw the shapes of the country to which their eyes were accustomed, and recognised the well-known landmarks, but it seemed that the distant hills were a trifle higher, and the grass which clothed them and stretched between was greener, was more velvety: that the trees were better clothed and had more of peace as they hung over the quiet ground.

But Mongan knew what had happened, and he smiled with glee as he watched his astonished companions, and he sniffed that balmy air as one whose nostrils remembered it.

"You had better come with me," he said.

"Where are we?" his wife asked.

"Why, we are here," cried Mongan; "where else should we be?"

He set off then, and the others followed, staring about them cautiously, and each man keeping a hand on the hilt of his sword.

"Are we in Faery?" the Flame Lady asked.

"We are," said Mongan.

When they had gone a little distance they came to a grove of ancient trees. Mightily tall and well-grown these trees were, and the trunk of each could not have been spanned by ten broad men. As they went among these quiet giants into the dappled obscurity and silence, their thoughts became grave, and all the motions of their minds elevated as though they must equal in greatness and dignity those ancient and glorious trees. When they passed through the grove they saw a lovely house before them, built of mellow wood and with a roof of bronze—it was like the dwelling of a king, and over the windows of the Sunny Room there was a balcony. There were ladies on this balcony, and when they saw the travellers approaching they sent messengers to welcome them.

Mongan and his companions were then brought into the house, and all was done for them that could be done for honoured guests. Everything within the house was as excellent as all without, and it was inhabited by seven men and seven women, and it was evident that Mongan and these people were well acquainted.

In the evening a feast was prepared, and when they had eaten well there was a banquet. There were seven vats of wine, and as Mongan loved wine he was very happy, and he drank more on that occasion than any one had ever noticed him to drink before.

It was while he was in this condition of glee and expansion that the Flame Lady put her arms about his neck and begged he would tell her the story of Duv Laca, and, being boisterous then and full of good spirits, he agreed to her request, and he prepared to tell the tale.

The seven men and seven women of the Fairy Palace then took their places about him in a half-circle; his own seven guards sat behind them; his wife, the Flame Lady, sat by his side; and at the back of all Cairidè his story-teller sat, listening with all his ears, and remembering every word that was uttered.

Chapter 5

Said Mongan:

In the days of long ago and the times that have disappeared for ever, there was one Fiachna Finn the son of Baltan, the son of Murchertach, the son of Muredach, the son of Eogan, the son of Neill. He went from his own country when he was young, for he wished to see the land of Lochlann, and he knew that he would be welcomed by the king of that country, for Fiachna's father and Eolgarg's father had done deeds in common and were obliged to each other.

He was welcomed, and he stayed at the Court of Lochlann in great ease and in the midst of pleasures.

It then happened that Eolgarg Mor fell sick and the doctors could not cure him. They sent for other doctors, but they could not cure him, nor could any one say what he was suffering from, beyond that he was wasting visibly before their eyes, and would certainly become a shadow and disappear in air unless he was healed and fattened and made visible.

They sent for more distant doctors, and then for others more distant still, and at last they found a man who claimed that he could make a cure if the king were supplied with the medicine which he would order.

"What medicine is that?" said they all.

"This is the medicine," said the doctor. "Find a perfectly white cow with red ears, and boil it down in the lump, and if the king drinks that rendering he will recover."

Before he had well said it messengers were going from the palace in all directions looking for such a cow. They found lots of cows which were nearly like what they wanted, but it was only by chance they came on the cow which would do the work, and that beast belonged to the most notorious and malicious and cantankerous female in Lochlann, the Black Hag. Now the Black Hag was not only those things that have been said; she was also whiskered and warty and one-eyed and obstreperous, and she was notorious and ill-favoured in many other ways also.

They offered her a cow in the place of her own cow, but she refused to give it. Then they offered a cow for each leg of her cow, but she would not accept that offer unless Fiachna went bail for the payment. He agreed to do so, and they drove the beast away.

They offered a cow for each leg of her cow, but she would not accept that offer unless Fiachna went bail for the payment

On the return journey he was met by messengers who brought news from Ireland. They said that the King of Ulster was dead, and that he, Fiachna Finn, had been elected king in the dead king's place. He at once took ship for Ireland, and found that all he had been told was true, and he took up the government of Ulster.

Chapter 6

A year passed, and one day as he was sitting at judgement there came a great noise from without, and this noise was so persistent that the people and suitors were scandalised, and Fiachna at last ordered that the noisy person should be brought before him to be judged.

It was done, and to his surprise the person turned out to be the Black Hag.

She blamed him in the court before his people, and complained that he had taken away her cow, and that she had not been paid the four cows he had gone bail for, and she demanded judgement from him and justice.

"If you will consider it to be justice, I will give you twenty cows myself," said Fiachna.

"I would not take all the cows in Ulster," she screamed.

"Pronounce judgement yourself," said the king, "and if I can do what you demand I will do it." For he did not like to be in the wrong, and he did not wish that any person should have an unsatisfied claim upon him.

The Black Hag then pronounced judgement, and the king had to fulfil it.

"I have come," said she, "from the east to the west; you must come from the west to the east and make war for me, and revenge me on the King of Lochlann."

Fiachna had to do as she demanded, and, although it was with a heavy heart, he set out in three days' time for Lochlann, and he brought with him ten battalions.

He sent messengers before him to Big Eolgarg warning him of his coming, of his intention, and of the number of troops he was bringing; and when he landed Eolgarg met him with an equal force, and they fought together.

In the first battle three hundred of the men of Lochlann were killed, but in the next battle Eolgarg Mor did not fight fair, for he let some venomous sheep out of a tent, and these attacked the men of Ulster and killed nine hundred of them.

So vast was the slaughter made by these sheep and so great the terror they caused, that no one could stand before them, but by great good luck there was a wood at hand, and the men of Ulster, warriors and princes and charioteers, were forced to climb up the trees, and they roosted among the branches like great birds, while the venomous sheep ranged below bleating terribly and tearing up the ground.

Fiachna Finn was also sitting in a tree, very high up, and he was disconsolate.

"We are disgraced!" said he.

"It is very lucky," said the man in the branch below, "that a sheep cannot climb a tree."

"We are disgraced for ever!" said the King of Ulster.

"If those sheep learn how to climb, we are undone surely," said the man below.

"I will go down and fight the sheep," said Fiachna. But the others would not let the king go.

"It is not right," they said, "that you should fight sheep."

"Some one must fight them," said Fiachna Finn, "but no more of my men shall die until I fight myself; for if I am fated to die, I will die and I cannot escape it, and if it is the sheep's fate to die, then die they will; for there is no man can avoid destiny, and there is no sheep can dodge it either."

"Praise be to god!" said the warrior that was higher up.

"Amen!" said the man who was higher than he, and the rest of the warriors wished good luck to the king.

He started then to climb down the tree with a heavy heart, but while he hung from the last branch and was about to let go, he noticed a tall warrior walking towards him. The king pulled himself up on the branch again and sat dangle-legged on it to see what the warrior would do.

The stranger was a very tall man, dressed in a green cloak with a silver brooch at the shoulder. He had a golden band about his hair and golden sandals on his feet, and he was laughing heartily at the plight of the men of Ireland.

Chapter 7

It is not nice of you to laugh at us," said Fiachna Finn.

"Who could help laughing at a king hunkering on a branch and his army roosting around him like hens?" said the stranger.

"Nevertheless," the king replied, "it would be courteous of you not to laugh at misfortune."

"We laugh when we can," commented the stranger, "and are thankful for the chance."

"You may come up into the tree," said Fiachna, "for I perceive that you are a mannerly person, and I see that some of the venomous sheep are charging in this direction. I would rather protect you," he continued, "than see you killed; for," said he lamentably, "I am getting down now to fight the sheep."

"They will not hurt me," said the stranger.

"Who are you?" the king asked.

"I am Manannán, the son of Lir."

Fiachna knew then that the stranger could not be hurt.

"What will you give me if I deliver you from the sheep?" asked Manannán.

"I will give you anything you ask, if I have that thing."

"I ask the rights of your crown and of your household for one day."

Fiachna's breath was taken away by that request, and he took a little time to compose himself, then he said mildly:

"I will not have one man of Ireland killed if I can save him. All that I have they give me, all that I have I give to them, and if I must give this also, then I will give this, although it would be easier for me to give my life."

"That is agreed," said Mannanán.

He had something wrapped in a fold of his cloak, and he unwrapped and produced this thing.

It was a dog.

Now if the sheep were venomous, this dog was more venomous still, for it was fearful to look at. In body it was not large, but its head was of a great size, and the mouth that was shaped in that head was able to open like the lid of a pot. It was not teeth which were in that head, but hooks and fangs and prongs. Dreadful was that mouth to look at, terrible to look into, woeful to think about; and from it, or from the broad, loose nose that waggled above it, there came a sound which no word of man could describe, for it was not a snarl, nor was it a howl, although it was both of these. It was neither a growl nor a grunt, although it was both of these; it was not a yowl nor a groan, although it was both of these: for it was one sound made up of these sounds, and there was in it, too, a whine and a yelp, and a long-drawn snoring noise, and a deep purring noise, and a noise that was like the squeal of a rusty hinge, and there were other noises in it also.

"The gods be praised!" said the man who was in the branch above the king.

"What for this time?" said the king.

"Because that dog cannot climb a tree," said the man.

And the man on a branch yet above him groaned out "Amen!"

"There is nothing to frighten sheep like a dog," said Manannán, "and there is nothing to frighten these sheep like this dog."

He put the dog on the ground then.

"Little dogeen, little treasure," said he, "go and kill the sheep."

And when he said that the dog put an addition and an addendum on to the noise he had been making before, so that the men of Ireland stuck their fingers into their ears and turned the whites of their eyes upwards, and nearly fell off their branches with the fear and the fright which that sound put into them.

It did not take the dog long to do what he had been ordered. He went forward, at first, with a slow waddle, and as the venomous sheep came to meet him in bounces, he then went to meet them in wriggles; so that in a while he went so fast that you could see nothing of him but a head and a wriggle. He dealt with the sheep in this way, a jump and a chop for each, and he never missed his jump and he never missed his chop. When he got his grip he swung round on it as if it was a hinge. The swing began with the chop, and it ended with the bit loose and the sheep giving its last kick. At the end of ten minutes all the sheep were lying on the ground, and the same bit was out of every sheep, and every sheep was dead.

"You can come down now," said Manannán.

"That dog can't climb a tree," said the man in the branch above the king warningly.

"Praise be to the gods!" said the man who was above him.

"Amen!" said the warrior who was higher up than that.

And the man in the next tree said:

"Don't move a hand or a foot until the dog chokes himself to death on the dead meat."

The dog, however, did not eat a bit of the meat. He trotted to his master, and Manannán took him up and wrapped him in his cloak.

"Now you can come down," said he.

"I wish that dog was dead!" said the king.

But he swung himself out of the tree all the same, for he did not wish to seem frightened before Manannán.

"You can go now and beat the men of Lochlann," said Manannán. "You will be King of Lochlann before nightfall."

"I wouldn't mind that," said the king.

"It's no threat," said Manannán.

The son of Lir turned then and went away in the direction of Ireland to take up his one-day rights, and Fiachna continued his battle with the Lochlannachs.

He beat them before nightfall, and by that victory he became King of Lochlann and King of the Saxons and the Britons.

He gave the Black Hag seven castles with their territories, and he gave her one hundred of every sort of cattle that he had captured. She was satisfied.

Then he went back to Ireland, and after he had been there for some time his wife gave birth to a son.

Chapter 8

You have not told me one word about Duv Laca," said the Flame Lady reproachfully.

“I am coming to that,” replied Mongan.

He motioned towards one of the great vats, and wine was brought to him, of which he drank so joyously and so deeply that all people wondered at his thirst, his capacity, and his jovial spirits.

“Now, I will begin again.”

Said Mongan:

There was an attendant in Fiachna Finn’s palace who was called An Dáv, and the same night that Fiachna’s wife bore a son, the wife of An Dáv gave birth to a son also. This latter child was called mac an Dáv, but the son of Fiachna’s wife was named Mongan.

“Ah!” murmured the Flame Lady.

The queen was angry. She said it was unjust and presumptuous that the servant should get a child at the same time that she got one herself, but there was no help for it, because the child was there and could not be obliterated.

Now this also must be told.

There was a neighbouring prince called Fiachna Duv, and he was the ruler of the Dal Fiatach. For a long time he had been at enmity and spiteful warfare with Fiachna Finn; and to this Fiachna Duv there was born in the same night a daughter, and this girl was named Duv Laca of the White Hand.

“Ah!” cried the Flame Lady.

“You see!” said Mongan, and he drank anew and joyously of the fairy wine.

In order to end the trouble between Fiachna Finn and Fiachna Duv the babies were affianced to each other in the cradle on the day after they were born, and the men of Ireland rejoiced at that deed and at that news. But soon there came dismay and sorrow in the land, for when the little Mongan was three days old his real father, Manannán the son of Lir, appeared in the middle of the palace. He wrapped Mongan in his green cloak and took him away to rear and train in the Land of Promise, which is beyond the sea that is at the other side of the grave.

When Fiachna Duv heard that Mongan, who was affianced to his daughter Duv Laca, had disappeared, he considered that his compact of peace was at an end, and one day he came by surprise and attacked the palace. He killed Fiachna Finn in that battle, and he crowned himself King of Ulster.

The men of Ulster disliked him, and they petitioned Manannán to bring Mongan back, but Manannán would not do this until the boy was sixteen years of age and well reared in the wisdom of the Land of Promise. Then he did bring Mongan back, and by his means peace was made between Mongan and Fiachna Duv, and Mongan was married to his cradle-bride, the young Duv Laca.

Chapter 9

One day Mongan and Duv Laca were playing chess in their palace. Mongan had just made a move of skill, and he looked up from the board to see if Duv Laca seemed as discontented as she had a right to be. He saw then over Duv Laca's shoulder a little black-faced, tufty-headed cleric leaning against the door-post inside the room.

"What are you doing there?" said Mongan.

"What are you doing there yourself?" said the little black-faced cleric.

"Indeed, I have a right to be in my own house," said Mongan.

"Indeed I do not agree with you," said the cleric.

"Where ought I be, then?" said Mongan.

"You ought to be at Dun Fiathac avenging the murder of your father," replied the cleric, "and you ought to be ashamed of yourself for not having done it long ago. You can play chess with your wife when you have won the right to leisure."

"But how can I kill my wife's father?" Mongan exclaimed.

"By starting about it at once," said the cleric.

"Here is a way of talking!" said Mongan.

"I know," the cleric continued, "that Duv Laca will not agree with a word I say on this subject, and that she will try to prevent you from doing what you have a right to do, for that is a wife's business, but a man's business is to do what I have just told you; so come with me now and do not wait to think about it, and do not wait to play any more chess. Fiachna Duv has only a small force with him at this moment, and we can burn his palace as he burned your father's palace, and kill him as he killed your father, and crown you King of Ulster rightfully the way he crowned himself wrongfully as a king."

"I begin to think that you own a lucky tongue, my black-faced friend," said Mongan, "and I will go with you."

He collected his forces then, and he burned Fiachna Duv's fortress, and he killed Fiachna Duv, and he was crowned King of Ulster.

Then for the first time he felt secure and at liberty to play chess. But he did not know until afterwards that the black-faced, tufty-headed person was his father Manannán, although that was the fact.

There are some who say, however, that Fiachna the Black was killed in the year 624 by the lord of the Scot's Dal Riada, Condad Cerr, at the battle of Ard Carainn; but the people who say this do not know what they are talking about, and they do not care greatly what it is they say.

Chapter 10

There is nothing to marvel about in this Duv Laca," said the Flame Lady scornfully. "She has got married, and she has been beaten at chess. It has happened before."

"Let us keep to the story," said Mongan, and, having taken some few dozen deep draughts of the wine, he became even more jovial than before. Then he recommenced his tale:

It happened on a day that Mongan had need of treasure. He had many presents to make, and he had not as much gold and silver and cattle as was proper for a king. He called his nobles together and discussed what was the best thing to be done, and it was arranged that he should visit the provincial kings and ask boons from them.

He set out at once on his round of visits, and the first province he went to was Leinster.

The King of Leinster at that time was Branduv, the son of Echach. He welcomed Mongan and treated him well, and that night Mongan slept in his palace.

When he awoke in the morning he looked out of a lofty window, and he saw on the sunny lawn before the palace a herd of cows. There were fifty cows in all, for he counted them, and each cow had a calf beside her, and each cow and calf was pure white in colour, and each of them had red ears.

When Mongan saw these cows, he fell in love with them as he had never fallen in love with anything before.

He came down from the window and walked on the sunny lawn among the cows, looking at each of them and speaking words of affection and endearment to them all; and while he was thus walking and talking and looking and loving, he noticed that some one was moving beside him. He looked from the cows then, and saw that the King of Leinster was at his side.

"Are you in love with the cows?" Branduv asked him.

"I am," said Mongan.

"Everybody is," said the King of Leinster.

"I never saw anything like them," said Mongan.

"Nobody has," said the King of Leinster.

"I never saw anything I would rather have than these cows," said Mongan.

"These," said the King of Leinster, "are the most beautiful cows in Ireland, and," he continued thoughtfully, "Duv Laca is the most beautiful woman in Ireland."

"There is no lie in what you say," said Mongan.

"Is it not a queer thing," said the King of Leinster, "that I should have what you want with all your soul, and you should have what I want with all my heart?"

"Queer indeed," said Mongan, "but what is it that you do want?"

"Duv Laca, of course," said the King of Leinster.

"Do you mean," said Mongan, "that you would exchange this herd of fifty pure white cows having red ears—"

"And their fifty calves," said the King of Leinster—

"For Duv Laca, or for any woman in the world?"

"I would," cried the King of Leinster, and he thumped his knee as he said it.

"Done," roared Mongan, and the two kings shook hands on the bargain.

Mongan then called some of his own people, and before any more words could be said and before any alteration could be made, he set his men behind the cows and marched home with them to Ulster.

Chapter 11

Duv Laca wanted to know where the cows came from, and Mongan told her that the King of Leinster had given them to him. She fell in love with them as Mongan had done, but there was nobody in the world could have avoided loving those cows: such cows they were! such wonders! Mongan and Duv Laca used to play chess together, and then they would go out together to look at the cows, and then they would go in together and would talk to each other about the cows. Everything they did they did together, for they loved to be with each other.

However, a change came.

One morning a great noise of voices and trampling of horses and rattle of armour came about the palace. Mongan looked from the window.

"Who is coming?" asked Duv Laca.

But he did not answer her.

"The noise must announce the visit of a king," Duv Laca continued.

But Mongan did not say a word.

Duv Laca then went to the window.

"Who is that king?" she asked.

And her husband replied to her then.

"That is the King of Leinster," said he mournfully.

"Well," said Duv Laca surprised, "is he not welcome?"

"He is welcome indeed," said Mongan lamentably.

"Let us go out and welcome him properly," Duv Laca suggested.

"Let us not go near him at all," said Mongan, "for he is coming to complete his bargain."

"What bargain are you talking about?" Duv Laca asked.

But Mongan would not answer that.

"Let us go out," said he, "for we must go out."

Mongan and Duv Laca went out then and welcomed the King of Leinster. They brought him and his chief men into the palace, and water was brought for their baths, and rooms were appointed for them, and everything was done that should be done for guests.

That night there was a feast, and after the feast there was a banquet, and all through the feast and the banquet the King of Leinster stared at Duv Laca with joy, and sometimes his breast was delivered of great sighs, and at times he moved as though in perturbation of spirit and mental agony.

"There is something wrong with the King of Leinster," Duv Laca whispered.

"I don't care if there is," said Mongan.

"You must ask what he wants."

"But I don't want to know it," said Mongan.

"Nevertheless, you musk ask him," she insisted.

So Mongan did ask him, and it was in a melancholy voice that he asked it.

"Do you want anything?" said he to the King of Leinster.

"I do indeed," said Branduv.

"If it is in Ulster I will get it for you," said Mongan mournfully.

"It is in Ulster," said Branduv.

Mongan did not want to say anything more then, but the King of Leinster was so intent and everybody else was listening and Duv Laca was nudging his arm, so he said:

"What is it that you do want?"

"I want Duv Laca."

"I want her too," said Mongan.

"You made your bargain," said the King of Leinster, "my cows and their calves for your Duv Laca, and the man that makes a bargain keeps a bargain."

"I never before heard," said Mongan, "of a man giving away his own wife."

"Even if you never heard of it before, you must do it now," said Duv Laca, "for honour is longer than life."

Mongan became angry when Duv Laca said that. His face went red as a sunset, and the veins swelled in his neck and his forehead.

"Do you say that?" he cried to Duv Laca.

"I do," said Duv Laca.

"Let the King of Leinster take her," said Mongan.

Chapter 12

Duv Laca and the King of Leinster went apart then to speak together, and the eye of the king seemed to be as big as a plate, so fevered was it and so enlarged and inflamed by the look of Duv Laca. He was so confounded with joy also that his words got mixed up with his teeth, and Duv Laca did not know exactly what it was he was trying to say, and he did not seem to know himself. But at last he did say something intelligible, and this is what he said:

"I am a very happy man," said he.

"And I," said Duv Laca, "am the happiest woman in the world."

"Why should you be happy?" the astonished king demanded.

"Listen to me," she said. "If you tried to take me away from this place against my own wish, one half of the men of Ulster would be dead before you got me and the other half would be badly wounded in my defence."

"A bargain is a bargain," the King of Leinster began.

"But," she continued, "they will not prevent my going away, for they all know that I have been in love with you for ages."

"What have you been in with me for ages?" said the amazed king.

"In love with you," replied Duv Laca.

"This is news," said the king, "and it is good news."

"But, by my word," said Duv Laca, "I will not go with you unless you grant me a boon."

"All that I have," cried Branduv, "and all that everybody has."

"And you must pass your word and pledge your word that you will do what I ask."

"I pass it and pledge it," cried the joyful king.

"Then," said Duv Laca, "this is what I bind on you."

"Light the yolk!" he cried.

"Until one year is up and out you are not to pass the night in any house that I am in."

"By my head and hand!" Branduv stammered.

"And if you come into a house where I am during the time and term of that year, you are not to sit down in the chair that I am sitting in."

"Heavy is my doom!" he groaned.

"But," said Duv Laca, "if I am sitting in a chair or a seat you are to sit in a chair that is over against me and opposite to me and at a distance from me."

"Alas!" said the king, and he smote his hands together, and then he beat them on his head, and then he looked at them and at everything about, and he could not tell what anything was or where anything was, for his mind was clouded and his wits had gone astray.

"Why do you bind these woes on me?" he pleaded.

"I wish to find out if you truly love me."

"But I do," said the king. "I love you madly and dearly, and with all my faculties and members."

"That is the way I love you," said Duv Laca. "We shall have a notable year of courtship and joy. And let us go now," she continued, "for I am impatient to be with you."

"Alas!" said Branduv, as he followed her. "Alas, alas!" said the King of Leinster.

Chapter 13

I think," said the Flame Lady, "that whoever lost that woman had no reason to be sad."

Mongan took her chin in his hand and kissed her lips.

"All that you say is lovely, for you are lovely," said he, "and you are my delight and the joy of the world."

Then the attendants brought him wine, and he drank so joyously of that and so deeply, that those who observed him thought he would surely burst and drown them. But he laughed loudly and with enormous delight, until the vessels of gold and silver and bronze chimed mellowly to his peal and the rafters of the house went creaking.

For (said he), Mongan loved Duv Laca of the White Hand better than he loved his life, better than he loved his honour. The kingdoms of the world did not weigh with him beside the string of her shoe. He would not look at a sunset if he could see her. He would not listen to a harp if he could hear her speak, for she was the delight of ages, the gem of time, and the wonder of the world till Doom.

She went to Leinster with the king of that country, and when she had gone Mongan fell grievously sick, so that it did not seem he could ever recover again; and he began to waste and wither, and he began to look like a skeleton, and a bony structure, and a misery.

Now this also must be known.

Duv Laca had a young attendant, who was her foster-sister as well as her servant, and on the day that she got married to Mongan, her attendant was married to mac an Dáv, who was servant and foster-brother to Mongan. When Duv Laca went away with the King of Leinster, her servant, mac an Dáv's wife, went with her, so there were two wifeless men in Ulster at that time, namely, Mongan the king and mac an Dáv his servant.

One day as Mongan sat in the sun, brooding lamentably on his fate, mac an Dáv came to him.

"How are things with you, master?" asked mac an Dáv.

"Bad," said Mongan.

"It was a poor day brought you off with Manannán to the Land of Promise," said his servant.

"Why should you think that?" inquired Mongan.

"Because," said mac an Dáv, "you learned nothing in the Land of Promise except how to eat a lot of food and how to do nothing in a deal of time."

"What business is it of yours?" said Mongan angrily.

"It is my business surely," said mac an Dáv, "for my wife has gone off to Leinster with your wife, and she wouldn't have gone if you hadn't made a bet and a bargain with that accursed king."

Mac an Dáv began to weep then.

"I didn't make a bargain with any king," said he, "and yet my wife has gone away with one, and it's all because of you."

"There is no one sorrier for you than I am," said Mongan.

"There is indeed," said mac an Dáv, "for I am sorrier myself."

Mongan roused himself then.

"You have a claim on me truly," said he, "and I will not have any one with a claim on me that is not satisfied. Go," he said to mac an Dáv, "to that fairy place we both know of. You remember the baskets I left there with the sod from Ireland in one and the sod from Scotland in the other; bring me the baskets and sods."

"Tell me the why of this?" said his servant.

"The King of Leinster will ask his wizards what I am doing, and this is what I will be doing. I will get on your back with a foot in each of the baskets, and when Branduv asks the wizards where I am they will tell him that I have one leg in Ireland and one leg in Scotland, and as long as they tell him that he will think he need not bother himself about me, and we will go into Leinster that way."

"No bad way either," said mac an Dáv.

They set out then.

Chapter 14

It was a long, uneasy journey, for although mac an Dáv was of stout heart and goodwill, yet no man can carry another on his back from Ulster to Leinster and go quick. Still, if you keep on driving a pig or a story they will get at last to where you wish them to go, and the man who continues putting one foot in front of the other will leave his home behind, and will come at last to the edge of the sea and the end of the world.

When they reached Leinster the feast of Moy Lifé was being held, and they pushed on by forced marches and long stages so as to be in time, and thus they came to the Moy of Cell Camain, and they mixed with the crowd that were going to the feast.

A great and joyous concourse of people streamed about them. There were young men and young girls, and when these were not holding each other's hands it was because their arms were round each other's necks. There were old, lusty women going by, and when these were not talking together it was because their mouths were mutually filled with apples and meat-pies. There were young warriors with mantles of green and purple and red flying behind them on the breeze, and when these were not looking disdainfully on older soldiers it was because the older soldiers happened at the moment to be looking at them. There were old warriors with yard-long beards flying behind their shoulders like wisps of hay, and when these were not nursing a broken arm or a cracked skull, it was because they were nursing wounds in their stomachs or their legs. There were troops of young women who giggled as long as their breaths lasted and beamed when it gave out. Bands of boys who whispered mysteriously together and pointed with their fingers in every direction at once, and would suddenly begin to run like a herd of stampeded horses. There were men with carts full of roasted meats. Women with little vats full of mead, and others carrying milk and beer. Folk of both sorts with towers swaying on their heads, and they dripping with honey. Children having baskets piled with red apples, and old women who peddled shell-fish and boiled lobsters. There were people who sold twenty kinds of bread, with butter thrown in. Sellers of onions and cheese, and others who supplied spare bits of armour, odd scabbards, spear handles, breastplate-laces. People who cut your hair or told your fortune or gave you a hot bath in a pot. Others who put a shoe on your horse or a piece of embroidery on your mantle; and others, again, who took stains off your sword or dyed your finger-nails or sold you a hound.

It was a great and joyous gathering that was going to the feast.

Mongan and his servant sat against a grassy hedge by the roadside and watched the multitude streaming past.

Just then Mongan glanced to the right whence the people were coming. Then he pulled the hood of his cloak over his ears and over his brow.

"Alas!" said he in a deep and anguished voice.

Mac an Dáv turned to him.

"Is it a pain in your stomach, master?"

"It is not," said Mongan.

"Well, what made you make that brutal and belching noise?"

"It was a sigh I gave," said Mongan.

"Whatever it was," said mac an Dáv, "what was it?"

"Look down the road on this side and tell me who is coming," said his master.

"It is a lord with his troop."

"It is the King of Leinster," said Mongan.

"The man," said mac an Dáv in a tone of great pity, "the man that took away your wife! And," he roared in a voice of extraordinary savagery, "the man that took away my wife into the bargain, and she not in the bargain."

"Hush," said Mongan, for a man who heard his shout stopped to tie a sandal, or to listen.

"Master," said mac an Dáv as the troop drew abreast and moved past.

"What is it, my good friend?"

"Let me throw a little, small piece of a rock at the King of Leinster."

"I will not."

"A little bit only, a small bit about twice the size of my head."

"I will not let you," said Mongan.

When the king had gone by mac an Dáv groaned a deep and dejected groan.

"Ocón!" said he. "Ocón-ío-go-deó!" said he.

The man who had tied his sandal said then:

"Are you in pain, honest man?"

"I am not in pain," said mac an Dáv.

"Well, what was it that knocked a howl out of you like the yelp of a sick dog, honest man?"

"Go away," said mac an Dáv, "go away, you flat-faced, nosy person."

"There is no politeness left in this country," said the stranger, and he went away to a certain distance, and from thence he threw a stone at mac an Dáv's nose, and hit it.

Chapter 15

The road was now not so crowded as it had been. Minutes would pass and only a few travellers would come, and minutes more would go when nobody was in sight at all.

Then two men came down the road: they were clerics.

"I never saw that kind of uniform before," said mac an Dáv.

"Even if you didn't," said Mongan, "there are plenty of them about. They are men that don't believe in our gods," said he.

"Do they not, indeed?" said mac an Dáv. "The rascals!" said he. "What, what would Manannán say to that?"

"The one in front carrying the big book is Tibraidè. He is the priest of Cell Camain, and he is the chief of those two."

"Indeed, and indeed!" said mac an Dáv. "The one behind must be his servant, for he has a load on his back."

The priests were reading their offices, and mac an Dáv marvelled at that.

"What is it they are doing?" said he.

"They are reading."

"Indeed, and indeed they are," said mac an Dáv. "I can't make out a word of the language except that the man behind says amen, amen, every time the man in front puts a grunt out of him. And they don't like our gods at all!" said mac an Dáv.

"They do not," said Mongan.

"Play a trick on them, master," said mac an Dáv.

Mongan agreed to play a trick on the priests.

He looked at them hard for a minute, and then he waved his hand at them.

The two priests stopped, and they stared straight in front of them, and then they looked at each other, and then they looked at the sky. The clerk began to bless himself, and then Tibraidè began to bless himself, and after that they didn't know what to do. For where there had been a road with hedges on each side and fields stretching beyond them, there was now no road, no hedge, no field; but there was a great broad river sweeping across their path; a mighty tumble of yellowy-brown waters, very swift, very savage; churning and billowing and jockeying among rough boulders and islands of stone. It was a water of villainous depth and of detestable wetness; of ugly hurrying and of desolate cavernous sound. At a little to their right there was a thin uncomely bridge that waggled across the torrent.

Tibraidè rubbed his eyes, and then he looked again.

"Do you see what I see?" said he to the clerk.

"I don't know what you see," said the clerk, "but what I see I never did see before, and I wish I did not see it now."

"I was born in this place," said Tibraidè, "my father was born here before me, and my grandfather was born here before him, but until this day and this minute I never saw a river here before, and I never heard of one."

"What will we do at all?" said the clerk. "What will we do at all?"

"We will be sensible," said Tibraidè sternly, "and we will go about our business," said he. "If rivers fall out of the sky what has that to do with you, and if there is a river here, which there is, why, thank God, there is a bridge over it too."

"Would you put a toe on that bridge?" said the clerk.

"What is the bridge for?" said Tibraidè.

Mongan and mac an Dáv followed them.

When they got to the middle of the bridge it broke under them, and they were precipitated into that boiling yellow flood.

Mongan snatched at the book as it fell from Tibraidè's hand.

"Won't you let them drown, master?" asked mac an Dáv.

"No," said Mongan, "I'll send them a mile down the stream, and then they can come to land."

Mongan then took on himself the form of Tibraidè and he turned mac an Dáv into the shape of the clerk.

"My head has gone bald," said the servant in a whisper.

"That is part of it," replied Mongan.

"So long as we know!" said mac an Dáv.

They went on then to meet the King of Leinster.

Chapter 16

They met him near the place where the games were played.

"Good my soul, Tibraidè!" cried the King of Leinster, and he gave Mongan a kiss. Mongan kissed him back again.

"Amen, amen," said mac an Dáv.

"What for?" said the King of Leinster.

And then mac an Dáv began to sneeze, for he didn't know what for.

"It is a long time since I saw you, Tibraidè," said the king, "but at this minute I am in great haste and hurry. Go you on before me to the fortress, and you can talk to the queen that you'll find there, she that used to be the King of Ulster's wife. Kevin Cochlach, my charioteer, will go with you, and I will follow you myself in a while."

The King of Leinster went off then, and Mongan and his servant went with the charioteer and the people.

Mongan read away out of the book, for he found it interesting, and he did not want to talk to the charioteer, and mac an Dáv cried amen, amen, every time that Mongan took his breath. The people who were going with them said to one another that mac an Dáv was a queer kind of clerk, and that they had never seen any one who had such a mouthful of amens.

But in a while they came to the fortress, and they got into it without any trouble, for Kevin Cochlach, the king's charioteer, brought them in. Then they were led to the room where Duv Laca was, and as he went into that room Mongan shut his eyes, for he did not want to look at Duv Laca while other people might be looking at him.

"Let everybody leave this room, while I am talking to the queen," said he; and all the attendants left the room, except one, and she wouldn't go, for she wouldn't leave her mistress.

Then Mongan opened his eyes and he saw Duv Laca, and he made a great bound to her and took her in his arms, and mac an Dáv made a savage and vicious and terrible jump at the attendant, and took her in his arms, and bit her ear and kissed her neck and wept down into her back.

"Go away," said the girl, "unhand me, villain," said she.

"I will not," said mac an Dáv, "for I'm your own husband, I'm your own mac, your little mac, your macky-wac-wac." Then the attendant gave a little squeal, and she bit him on each ear and kissed his neck and wept down into his back, and said that it wasn't true and that it was.

Chapter 17

But they were not alone, although they thought they were. The hag that guarded the jewels was in the room. She sat hunched up against the wall, and as she looked like a bundle of rags they did not notice her. She began to speak then.

"Terrible are the things I see," said she. "Terrible are the things I see."

Mongan and his servant gave a jump of surprise, and their two wives jumped and squealed. Then Mongan puffed out his cheeks till his face looked like a bladder, and he blew a magic breath at the hag, so that she seemed to be surrounded by a fog, and when she looked through that breath everything seemed to be different to what she had thought. Then she began to beg everybody's pardon.

"I had an evil vision," said she, "I saw crossways. How sad it is that I should begin to see the sort of things I thought I saw."

"Sit in this chair, mother," said Mongan, "and tell me what you thought you saw," and he slipped a spike under her, and mac an Dáv pushed her into the seat, and she died on the spike.

Just then there came a knocking at the door. Mac an Dáv opened it, and there was Tibraidè standing outside, and twenty-nine of his men were with him, and they were all laughing.

"A mile was not half enough," said mac an Dáv reproachfully.

The Chamberlain of the fortress pushed into the room and he stared from one Tibraidè to the other.

"This is a fine growing year," said he. "There never was a year when Tibraidès were as plentiful as they are this year. There is a Tibraidè outside and a Tibraidè inside, and who knows but there are some more of them under the bed. The place is crawling with them," said he.

Mongan pointed at Tibraidè.

"Don't you know who that is?" he cried.

"I know who he says he is," said the Chamberlain.

"Well, he is Mongan," said Mongan, "and these twenty-nine men are twenty-nine of his nobles from Ulster."

At that news the men of the household picked up clubs and cudgels and every kind of thing that was near, and made a violent and woeful attack on Tibraidè's men. The King of Leinster came in then, and when

he was told Tibraidè was Mongan he attacked them as well, and it was with difficulty that Tibraidè got away to Cell Camain with nine of his men and they all wounded.

The King of Leinster came back then. He went to Duv Laca's room.

"Where is Tibraidè?" said he.

"It wasn't Tibraidè was here," said the hag who was still sitting on the spike, and was not half dead, "it was Mongan."

"Why did you let him near you?" said the king to Duv Laca.

"There is no one has a better right to be near me than Mongan has," said Duv Laca, "he is my own husband," said she.

And then the king cried out in dismay:

"I have beaten Tibraidè's people." He rushed from the room.

"Send for Tibraidè till I apologise," he cried. "Tell him it was all a mistake. Tell him it was Mongan."

Chapter 18

Mongan and his servant went home, and (for what pleasure is greater than that of memory exercised in conversation?) for a time the feeling of an adventure well accomplished kept him in some contentment. But at the end of a time that pleasure was worn out, and Mongan grew at first dispirited and then sullen, and after that as ill as he had been on the previous occasion. For he could not forget Duv Laca of the White Hand, and he could not remember her without longing and despair.

It was in the illness which comes from longing and despair that he sat one day looking on a world that was black although the sun shone, and that was lean and unwholesome although autumn fruits were heavy on the earth and the joys of harvest were about him.

"Winter is in my heart," quoth he, "and I am cold already."

He thought too that some day he would die, and the thought was not unpleasant, for one half of his life was away in the territories of the King of Leinster, and the half that he kept in himself had no spice in it.

He was thinking in this way when mac an Dáv came towards him over the lawn, and he noticed that mac an Dáv was walking like an old man.

He took little slow steps, and he did not loosen his knees when he walked, so he went stiffly. One of his feet turned pitifully outwards, and the other turned lamentably in. His chest was pulled inwards, and his head was stuck outwards and hung down in the place where his chest should have been, and his arms were crooked in front of him with the hands turned wrongly, so that one palm was shown to the east of the world and the other one was turned to the west.

"How goes it, mac an Dáv?" said the king.

"Bad," said mac an Dáv.

"Is that the sun I see shining, my friend?" the king asked.

"It may be the sun," replied mac an Dáv, peering curiously at the golden radiance that dozed about them, "but maybe it's a yellow fog."

"What is life at all?" said the king.

"It is a weariness and a tiredness," said mac an Dáv. "It is a long yawn without sleepiness. It is a bee, lost at midnight and buzzing on a pane. It is the noise made by a tied-up dog. It is nothing worth dreaming about. It is nothing at all."

"How well you explain my feelings about Duv Laca," said the king.

"I was thinking about my own lamb," said mac an Dáv. "I was thinking about my own treasure, my cup of cheeriness, and the pulse of my heart." And with that he burst into tears.

"Alas!" said the king.

"But," sobbed mac an Dáv, "what right have I to complain? I am only the servant, and although I didn't make any bargain with the

King of Leinster or with any king of them all, yet my wife is gone away as if she was the consort of a potentate the same as Duv Laca is."

Mongan was sorry then for his servant, and he roused himself.

"I am going to send you to Duv Laca."

"Where the one is the other will be," cried mac an Dáv joyously.

"Go," said Mongan, "to Rath Descirt of Bregia; you know that place?"

"As well as my tongue knows my teeth."

"Duv Laca is there; see her, and ask her what she wants me to do."

Mac an Dáv went there and returned.

"Duv Laca says that you are to come at once, for the King of Leinster is journeying around his territory, and Kevin Cochlach, the charioteer, is making bitter love to her and wants her to run away with him."

Mongan set out, and in no great time, for they travelled day and night, they came to Bregia, and gained admittance to the fortress, but just as he got in he had to go out again, for the King of Leinster had been warned of Mongan's journey, and came back to his fortress in the nick of time.

When the men of Ulster saw the condition into which Mongan fell they were in great distress, and they all got sick through compassion for their king. The nobles suggested to him that they should march against Leinster and kill that king and bring back Duv Laca, but Mongan would not consent to this plan.

"For," said he, "the thing I lost through my own folly I shall get back through my own craft."

And when he said that his spirits revived, and he called for mac an Dáv.

"You know, my friend," said Mongan, "that I can't get Duv Laca back unless the King of Leinster asks me to take her back, for a bargain is a bargain."

"That will happen when pigs fly," said mac an Dáv, "and," said he, "I did not make any bargain with any king that is in the world."

"I heard you say that before," said Mongan.

"I will say it till Doom," cried his servant, "for my wife has gone away with that pestilent king, and he has got the double of your bad bargain."

Mongan and his servant then set out for Leinster.

When they neared that country they found a great crowd going on the road with them, and they learned that the king was giving a feast in honour of his marriage to Duv Laca, for the year of waiting was nearly out, and the king had sworn he would delay no longer.

They went on, therefore, but in low spirits, and at last they saw the walls of the king's castle towering before them. and a noble company going to and fro on the lawn.

Chapter 19

They sat in a place where they could watch the castle and compose themselves after their journey.

"How are we going to get into the castle?" asked mac an Dáv.

For there were hatchetmen on guard in the big gateway, and there were spearmen at short intervals around the walls, and men to throw hot porridge off the roof were standing in the right places.

"If we cannot get in by hook, we will get in by crook," said Mongan.

"They are both good ways," said mac an Dáv, "and whichever of them you decide on I'll stick by."

Just then they saw the Hag of the Mill coming out of the mill which was down the road a little.

Now the Hag of the Mill was a bony, thin pole of a hag with odd feet. That is, she had one foot that was too big for her, so that when she lifted it up it pulled her over; and she had one foot that was too small for her, so that when she lifted it up she didn't know what to do with it. She was so long that you thought you would never see the end of her, and she was so thin that you thought you didn't see her at all. One of her eyes was set where her

The Hag of the Mill was a bony, thin pole of a hag with odd feet

nose should be and there was an ear in its place, and her nose itself was hanging out of her chin, and she had whiskers round it. She was dressed in a red rag that was really a hole with a fringe on it, and she was singing "Oh, hush thee, my one love" to a cat that was yelping on her shoulder.

She had a tall skinny dog behind her called Brotar. It hadn't a tooth in its head except one, and it had the toothache in that tooth. Every few steps it used to sit down on its hunkers and point its nose straight upwards, and make a long, sad complaint about its tooth; and after that it used to reach its hind leg round and try to scratch out its tooth; and then it used to be pulled on again by the straw rope that was round its neck, and which was tied at the other end to the hag's heaviest foot.

There was an old, knock-kneed, raw-boned, one-eyed, little-winded, heavy-headed mare with her also. Every time it put a front leg forward it shivered all over the rest of its legs backwards, and when it put a hind leg forward it shivered all over the rest of its legs frontwards, and it used to give a great whistle through its nose when it was out of breath, and a big, thin hen was sitting on its croup.

Mongan looked on the Hag of the Mill with delight and affection.

"This time," said he to mac an Dáv, "I'll get back my wife."

"You will indeed," said mac an Dáv heartily, "and you'll get mine back too."

"Go over yonder," said Mongan, "and tell the Hag of the Mill that I want to talk to her."

Mac an Dáv brought her over to him.

"Is it true what the servant man said?" she asked.

"What did he say?" said Mongan.

"He said you wanted to talk to me."

"It is true," said Mongan.

"This is a wonderful hour and a glorious minute," said the hag, "for this is the first time in sixty years that any one wanted to talk to me. Talk on now," said she, "and I'll listen to you if I can remember how to do it.

Talk gently," said she, "the way you won't disturb the animals, for they are all sick."

"They are sick indeed," said mac an Dáv pityingly.

"The cat has a sore tail," said she, "by reason of sitting too close to a part of the hob that was hot. The dog has a toothache, the horse has a pain in her stomach, and the hen has the pip."

"Ah, it's a sad world," said mac an Dáv.

"There you are!" said the hag.

"Tell me," Mongan commenced, "if you got a wish, what it is you would wish for?"

The hag took the cat off her shoulder and gave it to mac an Dáv.

"Hold that for me while I think," said she.

"Would you like to be a lovely young girl?" asked Mongan.

"I'd sooner be that than a skinned eel," said she.

"And would you like to marry me or the King of Leinster?"

"I'd like to marry either of you, or both of you, or whichever of you came first."

"Very well," said Mongan, "you shall have your wish."

He touched her with his finger, and the instant he touched her all dilapidation and wryness and age went from her, and she became so beautiful that one dared scarcely look on her, and so young that she seemed but sixteen years of age.

"You are not the Hag of the Mill any longer," said Mongan, "you are Ivell of the Shining Cheeks, daughter of the King of Munster."

He touched the dog too, and it became a little silky lapdog that could nestle in your palm. Then he changed the old mare into a brisk, piebald palfrey. Then he changed himself so that he became the living image of Ae, the son of the King of Connaught, who had just been married to Ivell of the Shining Cheeks, and then he changed mac an Da'v into the likeness of Ae's attendant, and then they all set off towards the fortress, singing the song that begins:

My wife is nicer than any one's wife,
Any one's wife, any one's wife,
My wife is nicer than any one's wife,
Which nobody can deny.

Chapter 20

The doorkeeper brought word to the King of Leinster that the son of the King of Connaught, Ae the Beautiful, and his wife, Ivell of the Shining Cheeks, were at the door, that they had been banished from Connaught by Ae's father, and they were seeking the protection of the King of Leinster.

Branduv came to the door himself to welcome them, and the minute he looked on Ivell of the Shining Cheeks it was plain that he liked looking at her.

It was now drawing towards evening, and a feast was prepared for the guests with a banquet to follow it. At the feast Duv Laca sat beside the King of Leinster, but Mongan sat opposite him with Ivell, and Mongan put more and more magic into the hag, so that her cheeks shone and her eyes gleamed, and she was utterly bewitching to the eye; and when Branduv looked at her she seemed to grow more and more lovely and more and more desirable, and at last there was not a bone in his body as big as an inch that was not filled with love and longing for the girl.

Every few minutes he gave a great sigh as if he had eaten too much, and when Duv Laca asked him if he had eaten too much he said he had but that he had not drunk enough, and by that he meant that he had not drunk enough from the eyes of the girl before him.

At the banquet which was then held he looked at her again, and every time he took a drink he toasted Ivell across the brim of his goblet, and in a little while she began to toast him back across the rim of her cup, for he was drinking ale, but she was drinking mead. Then he sent a messenger to her to say that it was a far better thing to be the wife of the King of Leinster than to be the wife of the son of the King of Connaught, for a king is better than a prince, and Ivell thought that this was as wise a thing as anybody had ever said. And then he sent a message to say that he loved her so much that he would certainly burst of love if it did not stop.

Mongan heard the whispering, and he told the hag that if she did what he advised she would certainly get either himself or the King of Leinster for a husband.

"Either of you will be welcome," said the hag.

"When the king says he loves you, ask him to prove it by gifts; ask for his drinking-horn first."

She asked for that, and he sent it to her filled with good liquor; then she asked for his girdle, and he sent her that.

His people argued with him and said it was not right that he should give away the treasures of Leinster to the wife of the King of Connaught's son; but he said that it did not matter, for when he got the girl he would get his treasures with her. But every time he sent anything to the hag, mac an Dáv snatched it out of her lap and put it in his pocket.

"Now," said Mongan to the hag, "tell the servant to say that you would not leave your own husband for all the wealth of the world."

She told the servant that, and the servant told it to the king. When Branduv heard it he nearly went mad with love and longing and jealousy, and with rage also, because of the treasure he had given her and might not get back. He called Mongan over to him, and spoke to him very threateningly and ragingly.

"I am not one who takes a thing without giving a thing," said he.

"Nobody could say you were," agreed Mongan.

"Do you see this woman sitting beside me?" he continued, pointing to Duv Laca.

"I do indeed," said Mongan.

"Well," said Branduv, "this woman is Duv Laca of the White Hand that I took away from Mongan; she is just going to marry me, but if you will make an exchange, you can marry this Duv Laca here, and I will marry that Ivell of the Shining Cheeks yonder."

Mongan pretended to be very angry then.

"If I had come here with horses and treasure you would be in your right to take these from me, but you have no right to ask for what you are now asking."

"I do ask for it," said Branduv menacingly, "and you must not refuse a lord."

"Very well," said Mongan reluctantly, and as if in great fear; "if you will make the exchange I will make it, although it breaks my heart."

He brought Ivell over to the king then and gave her three kisses.

"The king would suspect something if I did not kiss you," said he, and then he gave the hag over to the king.

After that they all got drunk and merry, and soon there was a great snoring and snorting, and very soon all the servants fell asleep also, so that Mongan could not get anything to drink. Mac an Dáv said it was a great shame, and he kicked some of the servants, but they did not budge, and then he slipped out to the stables and saddled two mares. He got on one with his wife behind him and Mongan got on the other with Duv Laca behind him, and they rode away towards Ulster like the wind, singing this song:

The King of Leinster was married to-day,
Married to-day, married to-day,
The King of Leinster was married to-day,
And every one wishes him joy.

In the morning the servants came to waken the King of Leinster, and when they saw the face of the hag lying on the pillow beside the king, and her nose all covered with whiskers, and her big foot and little foot sticking away out at the end of the bed, they began to laugh, and poke one another in the stomachs and thump one another on the shoulders, so that the noise awakened the king, and he asked what was the matter with them at all. It was then he saw the hag lying beside him, and he gave a great screech and jumped out of the bed.

"Aren't you the Hag of the Mill?" said he.

"I am indeed," she replied, "and I love you dearly."

"I wish I didn't see you," said Branduv.

That was the end of the story, and when he had told it Mongan began to laugh uproariously and called for more wine. He drank this deeply, as though he was full of thirst and despair and a wild jollity, but when the Flame Lady began to weep he took her in his arms and caressed her, and said that she was the love of his heart and the one treasure of the world.

After that they feasted in great contentment, and at the end of the feasting they went away from Faery and returned to the world of men.

They came to Mongan's palace at Moy Linney, and it was not until they reached the palace that they found they had been away one whole year, for they had thought they were only away one night. They lived then peacefully and lovingly together, and that ends the story, but Brótiarna did not know that Mongan was Fionn.

The abbot leaned forward.

"Was Mongan Fionn?" he asked in a whisper.

"He was," replied Cairidè.

"Indeed, indeed!" said the abbot.

After a while he continued: "There is only one part of your story that I do not like."

"What part is that?" asked Cairidè.

"It is the part where the holy man Tibraidè was ill treated by that rap—by that—by Mongan."

Cairidè agreed that it was ill done, but to himself he said gleefully that whenever he was asked to tell the story of how he told the story of Mongan he would remember what the abbot said.